Collins

Work on your
Vocabulary
Advanced **C1**

Collins

HarperCollins Publishers
77-85 Fulham Palace Road
Hammersmith
London W6 8JB

First edition 2013

Reprint 10 9 8 7 6 5 4 3 2 1 0

© HarperCollins Publishers 2013

ISBN 978-0-00-749968-7

Collins® is a registered trademark of HarperCollins Publishers Limited

www.collinselt.com

A catalogue record for this book is available from the British Library

Typeset in India by Aptara

Printed in China by South China Printing Co.

The material in this book has been written by a team from Language Testing 123, a UK-based consultancy that specializes in English language assessment and materials. The units are by Sue Elliott and have been based on material from the Collins Corpus and the Collins COBUILD reference range. Word Finder boxes have been compiled by Rosalind Combley.

www.languagetesting123.co

Contents

Introduction

Welcome to *Work on your Vocabulary – Advanced (C1).*

Is this the right book for me?

This book, *Work on your Vocabulary – Advanced (C1)*, helps students to learn and practise English vocabulary at CEF level C1. This book is suitable for you to use if you are at CEF level C1, or just below.

So, what is CEF level C1? Well, there are six Common European Framework levels. They go up from A1 for beginners, A2, B1, B2, C1 and finally C2.

If the description below sounds like you, then this is probably the right book for you. If not, choose *Work on your Vocabulary – Upper Intermediate (B2)*, which is for study at a slightly lower level.

- I can understand the words and expressions when I read a wide range of texts and I can follow what almost everyone says, whether directly to me or on the TV and so on.
- I can use words and phrases to express my feelings, opinions and ideas quite fluently.
- I can adjust to different situations in using English, for example from academic to work-based to social situations.
- When I write or speak, I can use a range of different vocabulary, although I'm aware that there are gaps in my knowledge and I make mistakes from time to time.

What does this book contain?

This book contains 30 units to help you learn and practise important vocabulary for this advanced (C1) level.

Each unit gives you **explanations** and **definitions** of the words and expressions for the topic area, in the **Word Finder** boxes.

There is a series of **exercises** that give you useful practice in this particular area.

The **answers** to all the exercises are at the back of the book.

At the back of the book, you'll also find a list of all the words introduced in the book (the **Index**). Each word has the unit number next to it, so you can find it easily in the main part of the book.

The index also includes phonetics, to help you pronounce the words correctly. There is also a **pronunciation guide** to help you read and understand the phonetic symbols.

There are **Good to know!** boxes to help you to pay attention to important information about the words and expressions.

I'm a student: how can I use this book?

You can use this book in different ways. It depends on your needs, and the time that you have.

- If you have a teacher, he or she may give you some advice about using the book.

- If you are working alone, you may decide to study the complete book from beginning to end, starting with Unit 1 and working your way through to the end.

- You might find that it is better to choose which units you need to study first, which might not be the first units in the book. Take control of what you learn and choose the units you feel are most important for you.

- You may also decide to use the book for reference when you are not sure about a particular vocabulary topic.

- You can find what you want to learn about by looking in the **Contents** page.

- Please note that, if you do not understand something in one unit, you may need to study a unit earlier in the book for more explanation.

Study tips

1 Read the aim and introduction to the unit carefully.

2 Read the explanation. Sometimes, there is a short text or dialogue; sometimes there are tables of information; sometimes there are examples with notes. These are to help you understand the most important information about this area of vocabulary.

3 Don't read the explanation too quickly: spend time trying to understand it as well as you can. If you don't understand, read it again more slowly.

4 Do the exercises. Don't do them too quickly: think carefully about the answers. If you don't feel sure, look at the explanation and Word Finder box again. Write your answers in pencil, or, even better, on a separate piece of paper. (This means that you can do the exercises again later.)

5 Check your answers to the exercises in the back of the book.

6 If you get every answer correct, congratulations! Don't worry if you make some mistakes. Studying your mistakes is an important part of learning.

7 Look carefully at each mistake: can you now see why the correct answer is what it is?

8 Read the explanation and definitions again to help you understand.

9 Finally, if the unit includes a **Good to know!** box, then try really hard to remember what it says. It contains a special piece of information about the words and expressions.

10 Always return: come back and do the unit's exercises again a few days later. This helps you to keep the information in your head for longer.

I want to improve my vocabulary

Good! Only using one book won't be enough to really make your vocabulary improve. The most important thing is you!

Buy a good dictionary for your level. You could try the *Collins COBUILD Advanced Dictionary of English*.

Of course, you need to have a notebook, paper or electronic. Try these six techniques for getting the best from it.

- *Make it personal*: When you're learning a new word or expression, try to write some examples about yourself or people or places you know. It's easier to remember sentences about your life than someone else's! For example, *I have one older brother and two younger sisters*.

- *Look out*: Everything you read or hear in English may contain some examples of the new vocabulary you're learning. Try to notice these examples. Also, try to write down some of these examples, so that you can learn them.

- *Think aloud*: Practise saying the new words aloud. It helps you to remember them better. Also, pronunciation is very important; people need to understand you!

- *Everywhere you go*: Take your notebook with you. Use spare moments, such as when you're waiting for a friend to arrive. Read through your notes. Try to repeat things from memory. A few minutes here and there adds up to a useful learning system.

- *Take it further*: Don't just learn the examples in the book. Keep making your own examples, and learning those.

- *Don't stop*: It's really important to keep learning. If you don't keep practising, you won't remember for very long. Practise the new vocabulary today, tomorrow, the next day, a week later and a month later.

I'm a teacher: how can I use this book with my classes?

The content included has been very carefully selected by experts from Language Testing 123, using the Common European Framework for Reference, English Profile, the British Council Core Inventory, the Collins Corpus and the Collins COBUILD dictionaries range. As such, it represents a useful body of knowledge for students to acquire at this level. The language used is designed to be of effective general relevance and interest to any learner aged 14+.

The units use a range of exercise types to engage with students and to usefully practise what they have learnt from the explanation pages. There are enough exercises for each unit that it is not necessary for students to do all the exercises at one sitting. Rather, you may wish to return in later sessions to complete the remaining exercises.

The book will be a valuable self-study resource for students studying on their own. You can also integrate it into the teaching that you provide for your students.

The explanations and exercises, while designed for self-study, can be easily adapted by you to provide useful interactive work for your students in class.

You will probably use the units in the book to extend, back up or consolidate language work you are doing in class. This means you will probably make a careful choice about which unit to do at a particular time.

You may also find that you recommend certain units to students who are experiencing particular difficulty with specific language areas. Alternatively, you may use various units in the book as an aid to revision.

Lesson plan

1 Read the aim and introduction to the unit carefully: is it what you want your students to focus on? Make sure the students understand it.

2 Go through the explanation with your students. You may read this aloud to them, or ask them to read it silently to themselves. With a confident class, you could ask them to read some of it aloud.

3 If there is a dialogue, you could ask students to perform it. If there is a text, you could extend it in some way that makes it particularly relevant to your students. Certainly, you should provide a pronunciation model of focus language.

4 Take time over the explanation page, and check students' understanding. Use concept-checking questions.

5 Perhaps do the first exercise together with the class. Don't do it too quickly: encourage students to think carefully about the answers. If they don't feel sure, look together at the explanation again.

6 Now get students to do the other exercises. They can work alone, or perhaps in pairs, discussing the answers. This will involve useful speaking practice and also more careful consideration of the information. Tell students to write their answers in pencil, or, even better, on a separate piece of paper. (This means that they can do the exercises again later.)

7 Check their answers to the exercises in the back of the book. Discuss the questions and problems they have.

8 If the unit includes a **Good to know!** box, then tell students to try really hard to remember what it says. It contains a special piece of information about the words and expressions.

9 Depending on your class and the time available, there are different ways you could extend the learning. If one of the exercises is in the form of an email, you could ask your students to write a reply to it. If the exercises are using spoken language, then you can ask students to practise these as bits of conversation. They can re-write the exercises with sentences that are about themselves and each other. Maybe pairs of students can write an exercise of their own together and these can be distributed around the class. Maybe they can write little stories or dialogues including the focus language and perform these to the class.

10 Discuss with the class what notes they should make about the language in the unit. Encourage them to make effective notes, perhaps demonstrating this on the board for them, and/or sharing different ideas from the class.

11 Always return: come back and repeat at least some of the unit's exercises again a few days later. This helps your students to keep the information in their heads for longer.

Guide to word classes

All the words in **Word Finder** boxes have a word class. The table below gives you more information about each of these word classes.

Word class	Description
ADJECTIVE	An adjective is a word that is used for telling you more about a person or thing. You use adjectives to talk about appearance, colour, size, or other qualities, e.g. *He has got **short** hair.*
ADVERB	An adverb is a word that gives more information about when, how, or where something happens, e.g. *She went **inside**.*
CONJUNCTION	A conjunction is a word such as **and**, **but**, **if**, and **since**. Conjunctions are used for linking two words or two parts of a sentence together, e.g. *I'm tired **and** hungry.*
NOUN	A noun is a word that refers to a person, a thing, or a quality, e.g. *I live in the **city**.*
PHRASAL VERB	A phrasal verb consists of a verb and one or more particles, e.g. *When I go outside, I **put on** a warm coat.*
PHRASE	Phrases are groups of words that are used together and that have a meaning of their own, e.g. *I **would like** to get a new job.*
PREPOSITION	A preposition is a word such as **below**, **by**, **with**, or **from** that is always followed by a noun group or the **-ing** form of a verb. Prepositions are usually used to say where things are, e.g. *You can park **outside** the house.*
VERB	A verb is a word that is used for saying what someone or something does, or what happens to them, or to give information about them, e.g. *Can I **pay** by credit card?*

British and American English words and phrases

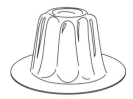

My grandmother makes the best **jelly** I've ever tasted!

Look at the examples of American English and their British English equivalents below.

American English	British English equivalent
mad	angry
emergency room	A & E (Accident & Emergency), casualty (department)
silverware, flatware	cutlery
driver's license	driving licence
fire department	fire brigade
overpass	flyover
give someone a ride	give someone a lift
purse	handbag
sick	ill
bug	insect
jelly	jam
highway	main road
buddy	mate, pal
math	Maths
license plate	number plate
deck of cards	pack of cards
grade school	primary school
real estate	property
swimsuit	swimming costume
closet	wardrobe

Good to know!

In some cases, American English will use a word or phrase which doesn't exist in British English, so there is no confusion over meaning, as in <u>overpass</u>.

However, there is potential for confusion when the same word exists in both varieties of English, but it means something different in each one, such as <u>purse</u>. *In American English, this is a handbag, but in British English, a* <u>purse</u> *is a small item that women keep their money in, often inside their handbag.*

Similarly, <u>silverware</u> *in British English means objects made from silver, such as ornamental cups and dishes, whereas in American English it refers to* <u>cutlery</u> *– knives, forks and spoons.*

angry / mad	ADJECTIVE When you are **angry**, you feel strong dislike or impatience about something.
casualty / emergency room	NOUN **Casualty** is the part of a hospital where people who have severe injuries or sudden illnesses are taken for emergency treatment.
cutlery / silverware, flatware	NOUN **Cutlery** consists of the knives, forks, and spoons that you eat your food with.
driving licence / driver's license	NOUN A **driving licence** is a card showing that you are qualified to drive because you have passed a driving test.
fire brigade / fire department	NOUN The **fire brigade** is an organization which has the job of putting out fires; used especially to refer to the people who actually fight the fires.
flyover / overpass	NOUN A **flyover** is a structure which carries one road over the top of another road.
give someone a lift / give someone a ride	PHRASE If you **give** someone **a lift** somewhere, you take them there in your car as a favour to them.
handbag / purse	NOUN A **handbag** is a small bag which a woman uses to carry things such as her money and keys in when she goes out.
ill / sick	ADJECTIVE Someone who is **ill** is suffering from a disease or a health problem.
insect / bug	NOUN An **insect** is a small animal that has six legs. Most insects have wings. Ants, flies, butterflies, and beetles are all insects.
jam / jelly	NOUN **Jam** is a thick sweet food that is made by cooking fruit with a large amount of sugar, and that is usually spread on bread.
main road / highway	NOUN A **main road** is an important road that leads from one town or city to another.
mate, pal / buddy	1 NOUN You can refer to someone's friends as their **mates**, especially when you are talking about a man and his male friends. 2 NOUN Some men use **mate** as a way of addressing other men when they are talking to them.
Maths / math	NOUN **Maths** is the study of numbers, quantities, or shapes.

Word Finder

number plate / **license plate**	NOUN A **number plate** is a sign on the front and back of a vehicle that shows its registration number.
pack of cards / deck of cards	NOUN A **pack of cards** is a complete set of playing cards.
primary school / **grade school**	NOUN A **primary school** is a school for children between the ages of 5 and 11.
property / **real estate**	NOUN **Property** is one or more buildings that someone owns and the land belonging to them.
swimming costume / **swimsuit**	NOUN A **swimming costume** is a piece of clothing that is worn for swimming, especially by women and girls.
wardrobe / closet	NOUN A **wardrobe** is a tall cupboard or cabinet in which you can hang your clothes.

(Word Finder sidebar label)

Exercise 1

Match the sentences containing words that mean the same in British and American English, as shown.

1 The evening's events made me very *angry*.

2 We drove over the motorway on the very busy *flyover*.

3 Forgetting her *handbag* was terrible, as it contained everything she needed.

4 It was impossible to sleep in the tent because of all the *insects* flying around.

5 The *wardrobe* is far too small to hold all the clothes.

6 A slice of toast spread thickly with *jam* is a good way to start the day.

a *Jelly* on bread makes a great breakfast.

b I felt *mad* because of what had happened.

c There isn't enough space in the *closet* for everything.

d There was extremely heavy traffic on the *overpass*.

e Our rest was disturbed by the fact that the air was full of *bugs*.

f Rachel found to her horror that she'd left her *purse* in the restaurant.

Exercise 2

Put the correct British English word or phrase in each gap, as shown.

| wardrobe | primary school | number plate | cutlery | casualty department | insect | main road | fire brigade |

1 flatware _____*cutlery*_____

2 license plate _____

3 closet _____

4 bug _____

5 emergency room _____

6 grade school _____

Exercise 3

For each question, tick the British word or phrase that means the same as the American word or phrase in *italics*, as shown.

1 The waiter set the tables with the best *silverware*.
   ☐ dishes
   ☐ crockery
   ☑ cutlery

2 Jed pulled onto the *highway* and drove off.
   ☐ motorway
   ☐ main road
   ☐ track

3 Steve has a great career ahead in *real estate*.
   ☐ commerce
   ☐ banking
   ☐ property

4 Ben kindly offered to give me a *ride* to the airport.
   ☐ ticket
   ☐ lift
   ☐ taxi fare

5 My *buddy* Sam is always having to help me out.
   ☐ partner
   ☐ colleague
   ☐ mate

6 Jack was taken to the *emergency room* as a precaution after his fall.
   ☐ health clinic
   ☐ doctor's surgery
   ☐ casualty department

Exercise 4

Write the British English equivalent of the American English word in brackets to complete each sentence, as shown.

1 There were so many _____*insects*_____ (bugs) flying around that I couldn't get to sleep.

2 Sarah didn't manage to get the _____ (license plate) of the guy who hit her car.

3 Phil was so _____ (mad) that he could hardly speak.

4 My daughter starts at _____ (grade school) soon.

5 Beth is hoping to study _____ (math) at university.

6 We gave Harry and his friends a _____ (ride) into the city.

Work and jobs

I'm a senior manager in a big company that manufactures steel products for the building industry. It was originally set up by a brilliant **entrepreneur** and operated with only a **skeleton staff**, but once the company began to do well, there was a **takeover** in the form of a management buyout. Since then we've gone from strength to strength. We recently put in a successful **tender** for a major contract, so, to meet our increased output needs, we advertised our **vacancies** in the local press, and we've since **recruited** a number of new people to expand our **workforce**, including two **supervisors** to oversee the work done on the factory floor.

I've **taken on** a **trainee** in management too, who is about to take on the job of **delivering** training to various departments. We also have a consultant working with us who's acting as our **adviser**. He looks at our training needs so that we can tailor the sessions we run.

I love my job and find it very **rewarding** – the perfect way to **earn a living**. Our **workplace** has a really lively atmosphere, and one of the biggest **perks** is that I have a lovely place to live, which is largely paid for by the company. I have a good level of **job security**, as **dismissals** here are practically unheard of, and generous **sick leave**. So I consider myself very lucky!

Word Finder

adviser	NOUN An **adviser** is an expert whose job is to give advice to another person or to a group of people.
deliver	VERB If you **deliver** something that you have promised to do, make, or produce, you do, make, or produce it.
dismissal	NOUN When an employee is dismissed from their job, you can refer to their **dismissal**.
earn/make/ do for a living	PHRASE If you **earn a living**, **make a living**, or do something **for a living**, you earn the money that you need to live in return for work that you do.
entrepreneur	NOUN An **entrepreneur** is a person who sets up businesses and business deals.
maternity leave	NOUN **Maternity leave** is time that a woman spends away from work because she is pregnant or has recently had a baby.
merger	NOUN A **merger** is the joining together of two separate companies or organizations so that they become one.
perk	NOUN **Perks** are special benefits that are given to people who have a particular job or belong to a particular group.
recruit	VERB If you **recruit** people for an organization, you select them and persuade them to join it or work for it.
rewarding	ADJECTIVE An experience or action that is **rewarding** gives you satisfaction or brings you benefits.
sick leave	NOUN **Sick leave** is time that a person spends away from work because of illness or injury.

Word Finder	**skeleton staff**	NOUN A **skeleton staff** is the smallest number of staff necessary in order to run an organization or service.
	supervisor	NOUN A **supervisor** is a person who supervises activities or people, especially workers or students.
	takeover	NOUN A **takeover** is the act of gaining control of a company by buying more of its shares than anyone else.
	take on	PHRASAL VERB If someone **takes** you **on**, they employ you.
	tender	NOUN A **tender** is a formal offer to supply goods or to do a particular job, and a statement of the price that you or your company will charge. If a contract is put out to tender, formal offers are invited. If a company wins a tender, their offer is accepted.
	trainee	NOUN A **trainee** is someone who is employed at a low level in a particular job in order to learn the skills needed for that job.
	workforce	1 NOUN The **workforce** is the total number of people in a country or region who are physically able to do a job and are available for work. 2 NOUN The **workforce** is the total number of people who are employed by a particular company.
	workplace	NOUN Your **workplace** is the place where you work.
	vacancy	NOUN A **vacancy** is a job or position which has not been filled.

Exercise 1

Put the correct word or phrase in each gap, as shown.

| tender | workplace | recruit | supervisor | workforce | taken on |

Local firm bucks national trend

Fulbright Metals is a long-established manufacturing company with a [1] _____*workforce*_____ of over 200 highly-skilled employees. Despite the economic downturn, the company has [2] _____ around 30 new workers in the last six months, having won the [3] _____ to supply specialized parts to a firm producing medical equipment. 'We [4] _____ most of our staff locally', says HR boss Elena Pritchard, 'and the company has a real family atmosphere.'

Michel Jeune, who works as a [5] _____ on the factory floor, agrees. 'I have been with Fulbright for over 20 years now, and the atmosphere is great. Any problems in the [6] _____ are dealt with promptly and fairly.'

15

Exercise 2

Rearrange the letters to find words, as shown. Use the definitions to help you.

1 nneeureetrrp _entrepreneur_ (someone who sets up businesses and business deals)

2 nolekest tffsa _____ (the smallest number of people necessary to run a business)

3 eentiar _____ (someone who is employed at a low level in an organization while they learn how to do a job)

4 ervakteo _____ (the act of gaining control of a company by buying more of its shares than anyone else)

5 osrrepusiv _____ (a person who makes sure that other employees are doing their jobs correctly)

6 tdrnee _____ (an offer to supply goods or services with a statement of what you will charge)

Exercise 3

Choose the correct word, as shown.

1 Our company has a **gap /** (**vacancy**) **/ necessity** for a senior accountant.

2 He works as an economic **professor / critic / adviser** to an employers' organization.

3 Repeated failure to meet targets led to her eventual **dismissal / failure / promotion**.

4 Several staff were made redundant after the **join / merger / cooperation** of the two companies.

5 She took six months' **maternity / motherhood / family** leave after the birth of her daughter.

6 These very short contracts mean that staff have almost no job **permanence / safety / security**.

Exercise 4

Match the sentence halves.

1 She made a claim of unfair	**a** dismissal against the company.
2 Cheap air travel is	**b** you see the children making progress.
3 She makes a living	**c** have to be put out to tender.
4 It's very rewarding when	**d** to staff in the financial sector.
5 All our cleaning contracts	**e** advising new bio-tech companies.
6 Our company delivers training	**f** one of the perks of the job.

Exercise 5

Complete the sentences by writing one word or phrase in each gap.

| recruit | rewarding | trainee | workplace | sick leave | takeover |

1 Unfortunately, Martina is on long-term _____ at the moment.

2 I find my work with asthma patients particularly _____.

3 Following the company's _____ of its main rival, it is one of the biggest suppliers of farm machinery in the UK.

4 We tend to _____ a lot of ex-army personnel.

5 Bullying in the _____ is taken very seriously.

6 She has got a place as a _____ accountant.

Travel and holidays

Memo

TO: All staff

FROM: Management

Please note that due to the extensive alterations now under way at the main railway station, and the resulting **congestion** on the access roads there, a number of staff members who **commute** into the city have been experiencing problems getting to the office. To ease staff **transportation** problems during this period, we have therefore arranged a temporary **shuttle** bus which will run from the stop before the main station and **drop** people outside the office. We trust staff will make full use of this service.

Hi!

This postcard is just to give you some idea of what we can see from the window of our **self-catering** apartment! We were lucky to find somewhere with a **vacancy** - it's quite busy here at this time of year. And you can just see the boat we've hired on the beach - we managed to **launch** that yesterday, and spent the rest of the day **aboard** the boat, **bound** for a deserted bay just along the coast, only normally accessible by a **track** - just glorious! We're going for an organized **trek** into the hills tomorrow, but we haven't been given the **itinerary** yet - I'll let you know how it goes! We're **moving on to** another resort soon, famous for its **eco-tourism**, so that'll be interesting!

See you soon,
Jen and Andy

Word Finder

aboard	PREPOSITION	If you are **aboard** a ship or plane, you are on it or in it.
bound for	PHRASE	If a vehicle or person is **bound for** a particular place, they are travelling towards it.
carriage	NOUN	A **carriage** is one of the separate, long sections of a train that carries passengers.
commute	VERB	If you **commute**, you travel a long distance every day between your home and your place of work.
congestion	NOUN	If there is **congestion** in a place, the place is extremely crowded and blocked with traffic or people.
diesel	NOUN	**Diesel** or diesel oil is the heavy oil used in a diesel engine.

drop	VERB If you **drop** someone or something somewhere, you take them somewhere, usually in a car or other vehicle, and leave them there.	
eco-tourism	NOUN **Eco-tourism** is the business of providing holidays and related services which are not harmful to the environment of the area.	
give way	PHRASE If a moving person, a vehicle, or its driver **gives way**, they slow down or stop in order to allow other people or vehicles to pass in front of them.	
itinerary	NOUN An **itinerary** is a plan of a journey, including the route and the places that you will visit.	
launch	VERB To **launch** a ship or a boat means to put it into water, often for the first time after it has been built.	
move on to	PHRASAL VERB If you **move on to** a place, you continue a journey and go to a different place.	
on the road	PHRASE If you are **on the road**, you are going on a long journey or a series of journeys by road.	
self-catering	ADJECTIVE If you go on a **self-catering** holiday or you stay in self-catering accommodation, you stay in a place where you have to make your own meals.	
shuttle	NOUN A **shuttle** is a plane, bus, or train which makes frequent journeys between two places.	
tank	NOUN A **tank** is a large military vehicle that is equipped with weapons and moves along on metal tracks that are fitted over the wheels.	
track	1 NOUN A **track** is a narrow road or path. 2 NOUN Railway **tracks** are the rails that a train travels along.	
transportation	1 NOUN **Transportation** refers to any type of vehicle that you can travel in or carry goods in. 2 NOUN **Transportation** is a system for taking people or goods from one place to another, for example using buses or trains.	
trek	1 VERB If you **trek** somewhere, you go on a journey across difficult country, usually on foot. 2 NOUN A **trek** is used to describe a long walking trip.	
vacancy	NOUN If there are **vacancies** at a building such as a hotel, some of the rooms are available to rent.	

Word Finder

Exercise 1

Choose the correct word.

1 This isn't our train. It's **bound / set / getting** for the north, not the south.

2 Can you **pick / drop / catch** us at the station, please?

3 I've had enough of this city – it's time to **bring / move / put** on.

4 Do not walk on the railway **road / lane / tracks** under any circumstances.

5 On a roundabout, you have to **give / allow / let** way to the right.

Exercise 2

For each question, tick the correct answer.

1 You have to cook for yourself if your holiday accommodation is
  ❏ self-service.
  ❏ self-catering.

2 I'd like a double room for tonight. Do you have any
  ❏ vacancies?
  ❏ congestion?

3 The captain of the ship would like to welcome you
  ❏ afloat.
  ❏ aboard.

4 In some parts of the desert, camels are the only method of
  ❏ vehicle.
  ❏ transportation.

5 The only way to get to our hotel was down a long, dusty and bumpy
  ❏ trek.
  ❏ track.

Exercise 3

Rearrange the letters to find words. Use the definitions to help you.

1 oec-orimuts _____ (environmentally-friendly provision of holiday services)

2 nakt _____ (a military vehicle, covered with armour and equipped with guns or rockets)

3 rciaraeg _____ (one of the sections of a train, which is joined to others)

4 anhluc _____ (when a boat or ship is put into water for the first time)

5 iselde _____ (heavy oil, used as fuel in engines)

6 nitirerya _____ (a plan of a journey, including the route and the places that will be visited)

Exercise 4

Complete the sentences by writing one word in each gap.

| shuttle | tank | vacancy | trek | bound | commute | diesel |

1 The ship was _____ for Italy.

2 The number of people who _____ to London every morning has dropped by 100,000.

3 We're going on a three-day _____ through the Atlas mountains when we arrive in Morocco.

4 The hotel _____ bus leaves for the airport every hour from the car park.

5 He drove a big, heavy old taxi that was built like a _____!

6 Do you know where you can get some _____ for your hire car?

Success and failure

Success

> **To whom it may concern,**
>
> Pedro Gonzalez has worked for this company for four years now, and during that time he has shown himself to be a very able young man. He **thrives** on challenge; through his own efforts he has greatly increased his level of **expertise** in his chosen field, and has **made** significant **headway** in both training and developing his team. I do not believe he has **fulfilled his full potential** quite yet, as I think he is still capable of achieving much more, given the right opportunities.

Failure

To: Dave
From: Andy
Subject: Project

Re. my last email, I'm seriously concerned now about the progress, or lack of it, on the project. The last meeting I had with Jon's team was a complete **fiasco** – they've all done their best, but I now see the budget we initially allocated wasn't adequate for them to do a good job. I suggest we free up some cash and put it at their disposal immediately. It may turn out to be a totally **abortive** attempt to save things, but if we don't, I reckon the whole thing risks **going belly up**.

Look at the table below. It shows which words and phrases have positive connotations, and which have negative ones.

Positive	Negative
climb the ladder	abortive
expertise	anti-climax
feat	come to nothing
full potential	comedown
get ahead	crash
make headway	fiasco
realization (of a dream)	flop
thrive	go belly up
	go pear-shaped

abortive	ADJECTIVE An **abortive** attempt or action is unsuccessful.
anticlimax	NOUN You can describe something as an **anticlimax** if it disappoints you because it happens after something that was very exciting, or because it is not as exciting as you expected.
climb the ladder	PHRASE If you **climb the ladder**, you progress to a higher level in an organization, career, or society.
comedown	NOUN If you say that something is a **comedown**, you think that it is not as good as something else that you have just done or had.
come to nothing	PHRASE If something **comes to nothing**, it does not produce any successful result.
crash	1 VERB If a business or financial system **crashes**, it fails suddenly, often with serious effects. 2 NOUN **Crash** is also a noun.
expertise	NOUN **Expertise** is special skill or knowledge that is acquired by training, study, or practice.
feat	NOUN If you refer to an action, or the result of an action, as a **feat**, you admire it because it is an impressive and difficult achievement.
fiasco	NOUN If you describe an event or attempt to do something as a **fiasco**, you are emphasizing that it fails completely.
flop	1 NOUN If something is a **flop**, it is completely unsuccessful. 2 VERB If something **flops**, it is completely unsuccessful.
fulfil your full potential	PHRASE If someone **fulfils** their **full potential**, they achieve all the success that they are capable of with the abilities or qualities that they have.
get ahead	PHRASAL VERB If you **get ahead**, you succeed in your career.
go belly up	PHRASE If a project or company **goes belly up**, it fails completely.
go pear-shaped	PHRASE If a situation **goes pear-shaped**, bad things start happening.
let-down	NOUN A **let-down** is a disappointment, usually because something has not happened in the way in which you expected or hoped it would happen.
make headway	PHRASE If you **make headway**, you progress towards achieving something.
prosper	VERB If people or businesses **prosper**, they are successful and make money.
realization	NOUN The **realization** of a dream is the act of making something that you wanted and imagined actually happen.
thrive	1 VERB If someone or something **thrives**, they do well and are successful, healthy, or strong. 2 VERB If you say that someone **thrives**, on a particular situation, you mean that they enjoy it or that they can deal with it very well, especially when other people find it unpleasant or difficult.

Word Finder

Exercise 1

Match the two parts.

1 an abortive   **a** potential
2 fulfil   **b** attempt
3 go   **c** ahead
4 come   **d** belly up
5 get   **e** to nothing
6 make   **f** headway

Exercise 2

Find the words or phrases that do not belong, as shown.

1 **Words that go with 'realize'**

   a dream   potential   (an assumption)

2 **Words that go with 'make'**

   progress   advance   headway

3 **Words that go with 'go'**

   pear-shaped   belly up   letdown

4 **Words that go with 'fulfil'**

   change   ambition   potential

5 **Words normally used to suggest failure**

   fiasco   feat   flop

6 **Words normally used to suggest something positive**

   go pear-shaped   to thrive   expertise

Exercise 3

Put the correct word in each gap.

comes | expertise | flop | letdown | loser | potential

Film review

Absence is a funny sort of film – and I don't mean 'funny ha ha'! Despite the undeniable
[1] _____ of the director and the track record of the scriptwriter, it's a film that
goes nowhere – [2] _____ to nothing – has no real focus. I'd been expecting great
things from the cast too, but it was a real [3] _____ when I realized they didn't have
interesting enough characters to play. Jed Brocklehurst plays a [4] _____ who thinks
he can turn his life around by finding love: I mean, is that a plot? It's such a pity that the roles
didn't allow any of the actors to reach their full [5] _____. I'm sorry to say it but I'll
have to put this film into the [6] _____ category!

Exercise 4

Put the correct word in each gap.

| nothing | expertise | fiasco | thriving | crash | prosper | abortive |

Hi Katarina,

I must just email you and let you know about that meeting I went to at work today. It was
a pathetic, [1] _____ attempt to get the staff to accept a reduction in salary. The
director, James Hammond, told us that the company was in bad shape and that all his attempts
to get more contracts had come to [2] _____. It's awful when you think that just
two years ago it was a [3] _____ company – but that was before the stock market
[4] _____. Anyway, the staff stuck to their guns and argued that there was still a
demand for their particular area of [5] _____, and if we all worked together the
company could grow and [6] _____ once more. Hammond got really frustrated and
started shouting – the whole meeting was a [7] _____ *fiasco* ___!

Exercise 5

Are the highlighted words and phrases correct or incorrect in the sentences?

1 Learning to snowboard at the age of 65 is no mean **feat** ☑.
2 He **thrives** ☐ on hard work.
3 After a poor box office performance, the musical was described as a **drop** ☐ by all the critics.
4 We seem to be making little **headlight** ☐ with this problem.
5 When the presents I'd ordered online didn't arrive on time, despite promises from the retailer,
   it was a real **get-down** ☐.
6 After the company he ran for five years collapsed, Tom found working for someone else again
   quite a **comedown** ☐.
7 My plans all went **banana-shaped** ☐ when Hugo refused to invest in the scheme.

Exercise 6

**Complete the sentences by writing one word in each gap, as shown. The first letter of the
missing word has been given.**

1 You will never _____ *fulfil* _____ (f) your true potential if you don't go to drama school.
2 Sergei was ambitious and ruthless. He _____ (c) the company ladder without
   giving a second thought to others.
3 The ending of the novel is a terrible _____ (a) because you think something
   momentous is going to happen and it doesn't.
4 Ingrid got _____ (a) by studying hard and working hard – there's no mystery to it.
5 It's no mean _____ (f) to run a business and bring up three children at the
   same time.
6 Are you making any _____ (h) with sorting out the student timetables for
   next year?

5

Services

The **amenities** in my town aren't bad. There are plenty of places for entertainment, including some reasonable restaurants and a leisure centre. There's a **one-stop shop** near my home, too, open all hours, so that's handy – although it doesn't do wonders for my chocolate **consumption**! It's also a **neighbourhood watch** area, so there's a very low crime rate.

For me, though, what **epitomizes** this town is the expression 'middle-of-the-road'. The restaurants are OK, but not that special and the cinema seems to show only the most popular films – nothing art-house. But then you do get a **complimentary** drink with your popcorn there, so I'm not complaining!

Look at the following words and phrases that are associated with different service providers, such as banks, shops, local authorities and places of entertainment.

Bank	Local authority	Leisure centre
bank charges	waste management	extreme sports centre
overdraft	traffic management	multiplex cinema
savings account	drop-in centre	
current account		
deposit account		
withdraw (money)		

amenities	NOUN **Amenities** are things such as shops or sports facilities that are provided for people's convenience, enjoyment, or comfort.
bank charges	NOUN **Bank charges** are amounts of money that you have to pay your bank for services such as withdrawing money.
beverage	NOUN A **beverage** is a drink.
complimentary	ADJECTIVE A **complimentary** meal or drink is given to you free.
consumption	1 NOUN The **consumption** of fuel or natural resources is the amount of them that is used or the act of using them.
	2 NOUN **Consumption** is the act of buying and using things.
courtesy	1 NOUN **Courtesy** is politeness, respect, and consideration for others.
	2 ADJECTIVE Services that are provided **courtesy** of a company are provided free of charge by an organization to its customers, or to the general public.
current account	NOUN A **current account** is a personal bank account which you can take money out of at any time, and which does not earn much interest.
drop-in centre	NOUN A **drop-in centre** is a place where you can visit without making an appointment to receive information, advice or a service.

Word Finder

embody	VERB To **embody** an idea or quality means to be a symbol or expression of that idea or quality.
encapsulate	VERB To **encapsulate** particular facts or ideas means to represent all their most important aspects in a very small space or in a single object or event.
epitomize	VERB If you say that something or someone **epitomizes** a particular thing, you mean that they are a perfect example of it.
extreme sports centre	NOUN An **extreme sports centre** is a place where people can take part in exciting and dangerous activities such as climbing or snowboarding.
local authority	NOUN A **local authority** is an organization that is officially responsible for all the public services and facilities in a particular area.
multiplex cinema	NOUN A **multiplex cinema** is a cinema complex with six or more screens.
neighbourhood watch	NOUN A **neighbourhood watch** is an organized group of people who live in the same area and try to prevent crime in the area by watching and protecting one another's homes.
one-stop shop	NOUN A **one-stop shop** is a single place or company where you can buy everything you need for a particular purpose.
overdraft	NOUN If you have an **overdraft**, you have spent more money than you have in your bank account, and so you are in debt to the bank.
savings / deposit account	NOUN A **savings account** or **deposit account** is a bank account in which you leave money for a long time and which earns interest.
traffic management	NOUN **Traffic management** is the activity of controlling how vehicles move around a city or area in a way that is safe and efficient.
waste management	NOUN **Waste management** is the job of removing material that is no longer wanted by households or industries and getting rid of it safely.
withdraw	VERB If you **withdraw** money from a bank account, you take it out of that account.

Word Finder

Exercise 1

Put the correct word or phrase in each gap.

> local authority | amenities | courtesy | encapsulates | multiplex cinema | traffic management

Overall, I think this town is a good place to live. There are plenty of [1] _____,
such as good shops, a swimming pool and even a [2] _____.

By and large, the [3] _____ does a good job of running things. The only
thing that isn't so good is the [4] _____ – in summer when there are lots of
tourists here, the roads become very congested.

Despite this, tourism is very important to us and visitors can be sure of being
treated with [5] _____. In fact, if I had to choose one word that
[6] _____ this town, I think it would be 'friendly'.

Exercise 2

For each question, tick the correct answer.

1 A complimentary drink
- ❏ tastes very nice.
- ❏ makes you feel good.
- ❏ is free.

2 The amenities of a place are
- ❏ the buildings in it.
- ❏ its surroundings.
- ❏ the useful features that people can use there.

3 A beverage is
- ❏ a formal word for a drink.
- ❏ a type of bank account.
- ❏ a light snack.

4 If someone treats you with courtesy, they
- ❏ help you.
- ❏ are polite to you.
- ❏ give you a free gift.

5 If something epitomizes a particular thing,
- ❏ it is damaged by it.
- ❏ it is a perfect example of it.
- ❏ it is an influence on it.

6 An overdraft is an agreement with your bank
- ❏ that allows you to spend more money than you have in your account.
- ❏ that allows you to pay back a loan with small, regular payments.
- ❏ that stops you from spending more than a particular amount.

Exercise 3

Complete the sentences by writing one word or phrase in each gap.

| drop-in centre | consumption | beverages | waste management | amenities | extreme sports centre |

1 The local authority has contracted its _____ and recycling services to a private company.

2 We do not allow _____ to be taken into the theatre.

3 He works at a _____ for people who need advice on how to manage their debts.

4 As a society, our _____ of plastic bags is way too high.

5 We were able to use most of the hotel's _____.

6 The new _____ offers high ropes, kitesurfing and bungee-jumping.

Exercise 4

Choose the correct word or phrase.

1 I changed to a different bank that had lower bank **expenses / charges / fees**.

2 We run a drop-in **store / office / centre** where people can get free health checks.

3 Her parents asked the bank to raise their overdraft **limit / border / maximum**.

4 He decided to keep a record of his **money / rent / fuel consumption**.

5 We are thinking of starting a neighbourhood **view / watch / safety** scheme here.

6 She went to the ATM to **withdraw / overdraw / extract** some money.

Exercise 5

Are the highlighted words correct or incorrect in this text?

Fed up with your current bank? Why not move to the bank that works for *you*? At YourBank, you will never be caught out by **hidden** ❑ bank charges. In fact, if you **enter** ❑ a savings account with us, we pay one of the highest interest rates around. And not only that, we pay interest on **actual** ❑ accounts too!

If you sometimes need a little extra at the end of the month, we will be happy to set up an overdraft **facility** ❑ for you. Every new customer gets a debit card immediately, enabling them to withdraw their **account** ❑ wherever they are. With competitive mortgages and travel services too, YourBank **provides** ❑ a one-stop shop for all your banking needs.

Exercise 6

Put each sentence into the correct order.

1 receive a / with a / new customers / complimentary consultation / personal trainer / all our / .

_____

2 a more efficient / upgrading to / reduce your / boiler can / energy consumption / help to / .

_____

3 innovative approach / that embodies / our company's / a new logo / to design / we want / .

_____

4 in an honest / we try always / manner that epitomizes / to operate / the service we offer / and professional / . _____

_____

5 by every / member of staff / with unfailing courtesy / I came into / I was treated / contact with / .

_____

6 good food, attentive / pleasant surroundings / amenities such as / of the package / staff and / are all part / . _____

_____

6

Register – formal vs. informal

There are a number of different words in English that mean the same thing. However, your choice of which one to use will depend on the register you are speaking or writing in.

Formal / neutral

> **Dan** I want to go into town tonight – have some **food** in my favourite restaurant ... but I haven't got much **money**. So please don't **get angry** if I ask you this, but could I possibly **borrow** some from you?
>
> **Michelle** Yes, of course. That's not a problem.

Informal / slang

> **Dan** I want to go into town tonight – have some **nosh** in my **fave** restaurant ... but I'm out of **dosh**. Don't **go ballistic** if I ask you this, but can I **scrounge** some off you?
>
> **Michelle** Sure – no worries.

Look at the table below. It shows what register you are likely to be speaking or writing in when you use each word or expression.

Formal	Neutral	Very informal (slang)
amelioration	improvement	
	borrow	scrounge
conceive	think up	
	courage	guts
denote	stand for	
deteriorate	get worse	
	disappointed	gutted
	doctor	quack
	food	nosh, grub
frequent	go to	
	get angry	go ballistic
go amiss	go wrong	go pear-shaped
	money	dosh, readies, dough
negate	wipe out	
notwithstanding	despite this	
repast	meal	
	terrible	lousy
thereby	in this way	
trigger	cause	
whereby	by which means, by which method	

amelioration / improvement	NOUN If there is an **amelioration** in something, it gets better or easier in some way.
borrow / scrounge	1 VERB If you **borrow** something that belongs to someone else, you take it or use it for a period of time, usually with their permission. 2 VERB If you **borrow** money from someone or from a bank, they give it to you and you agree to pay it back at some time in the future.
conceive / think up	VERB / PHRASAL VERB If you **conceive** a plan or idea, you think of it and work out how it can be done.
courage / guts	NOUN **Courage** is the quality shown by someone who decides to do something difficult or dangerous, even though they may be afraid.
denote / stand for	1 VERB / PHRASAL VERB What a symbol **denotes** is what it represents. 2 VERB / PHRASAL VERB What a word or name **denotes** is what it means or refers to.
deteriorate / get worse	VERB / PHRASE If something **deteriorates**, it becomes worse in some way.
disappointed / gutted	ADJECTIVE If you are **disappointed**, you are sad because something has not happened or because something is not as good as you had hoped.
doctor / quack	NOUN A **doctor** is someone who is qualified in medicine and treats people who are ill.
food / nosh, grub	NOUN **Food** is what people and animals eat.
frequent / go to	VERB / PHRASAL VERB If someone **frequents** a place, they visit it.
go amiss / go wrong / go pear-shaped	PHRASE If something **goes amiss**, it goes wrong.
go ballistic / get angry	PHRASE If someone **goes ballistic**, they get very angry.
money / dosh, readies, dough	NOUN **Money** is the coins or bank notes that you use to buy things, or the sum that you have in a bank account.
negate / wipe out	1 VERB / PHRASAL VERB If one thing **negates** another, it causes that other thing to lose the effect or value that it had. 2 VERB / PHRASAL VERB If someone **negates** something, they say that it does not exist.
notwithstanding / despite	PREPOSITION If something is true **notwithstanding** something else, it is true in spite of that other thing.
repast / meal	NOUN A **repast** is a meal.
terrible / lousy	1 ADJECTIVE If you feel **terrible**, you feel extremely ill or unhappy. If you tell someone that they look **terrible**, you mean that they look as if they are extremely ill or unhappy. 2 ADJECTIVE If something is **terrible**, it is very bad or of very poor quality.

Word Finder

Word Finder	thereby / in this way	ADVERB / PHRASE You use **thereby** to introduce an important result or consequence of the event or action you have just mentioned.
	trigger / cause	NOUN If something acts as a **trigger** for another thing such as an illness, event, or situation, the first thing causes the second thing to begin to happen or exist.
	whereby / by which	CONJUNCTION / PHRASE A system or action **whereby** something happens, is one that makes that thing happen.

Exercise 1

Find the words or phrases that do not belong, as shown.

1	**bad**	terrible	lousy	gutted
2	**food**	grub	guts	nosh
3	**go amiss**	go wrong	go ballistic	go pear-shaped
4	**money**	repast	dosh	readies

Exercise 2

Match the two parts.

1 That doctor doesn't know what he's doing.

2 She was very disappointed not to have made the team.

3 We often frequent that café.

4 He borrowed £30 from me, again.

5 He's got a lot of courage, that guy.

6 She's deteriorated overnight.

a He's always scrounging.

b She's definitely got worse.

c He's got real guts.

d We go there most lunchtimes.

e He's a quack.

f She was gutted.

Exercise 3

Decide if the pairs of sentences have the same meaning.

1 **A** She conceived the plan while sailing across the Channel.
  B She thought up the plan when she was sailing across the Channel.

2 **A** Steve has an intense dislike for George, notwithstanding their similar political views.
  B Steve hates George, because the two of them have differing political opinions.

3 **A** Taking vitamin supplements can lead to the amelioration of this skin condition.
  B This skin condition will show improvement with the taking of vitamins.

4 **A** They have devised a traffic flow system whereby people share private transport.
  B By avoiding the use of private transport, the traffic system flows better.

5 **A** I'm fairly certain it was cleaning out the dusty attic that triggered his asthma attack.
  B I think his asthma attack was caused by cleaning out the dusty attic.

Exercise 4

Rearrange the letters to find words. Use the definitions to help you.

1 stepar _____ (meal)

2 gnnidttasowhtin _____ (despite, in spite of)

3 rweyebh _____ (by which means/method)

4 eetgna _____ (wipe out)

5 neeodt _____ (stand for)

6 ybhreet _____ (in this way)

Exercise 5

Put the correct word or phrase in each gap.

| grub | ballistic | scrounging | going pear-shaped | guts | lousy | dosh | gutted |

Hi guys!

Having a fab time at the festival – wish you were here! Arrived a bit late and missed Jim's favourite band – he was ¹_____. Back to his cheerful self again now though. Steph went ²_____ at Neil when she found out he'd left her boots at home – the weather's awful and it's really muddy. The ³_____'s good – tasty and cheap – we've hardly used the barbecue we brought. Tilly's ⁴_____ as usual because she didn't bring enough ⁵_____. She needs to get a better job and start paying for herself! Pete got up on stage and joined in the singing – he's got ⁶_____, that one!

See you next week,

Trix

Exercise 6

Which sentences are correct?

1 What does LASER stand on? I never remember, no matter how many times I ask. ❑

2 A bunch of us were planning to make a bonfire on the beach, but it's all gone pear-shaped because health and safety have interfered. ❑

3 Bob, the dog, went ballistic overnight and passed away early the next morning. ❑

4 The company negated her contract when they found out she'd lied about her experience. ❑

5 The plan is to save more water, thereby avoiding such frequent shortages. ❑

6 This food is absolutely deteriorating. I can't believe they have the cheek to serve it. ❑

7

Feelings

My younger brother Nils had seemed completely **complacent** about his exams – he didn't seem to have done much work, and appeared to be totally **indifferent** to what grades he'd get. So imagine the **disbelieving** looks on our faces when he got all As!! Nils didn't react much, really – just gave us the same **mischievous** grin I always remember from when he was small!

Look at the table below. It shows the contexts in which the different adjectives in the unit might be used.

Happiness, confidence	Stupidity	Fear	Thoughtfulness	Negative feelings towards others	Sadness
blissful	idiotic	trapped	meditative	bitter	grief-stricken
self-assured	sheepish	threatened		enraged	homesick
hysterical		hysterical		nasty	lovesick
				revengeful	hysterical
				smug	

<table>
<tr><td rowspan="11">Word Finder</td><td>bitter</td><td>ADJECTIVE If someone is bitter after a disappointing experience or after being treated unfairly, they continue to feel angry about it.</td></tr>
<tr><td>blissful</td><td>ADJECTIVE A blissful situation or period of time is one in which you are extremely happy.</td></tr>
<tr><td>complacent</td><td>ADJECTIVE A complacent person is very pleased with themselves or feels that they do not need to do anything about a situation, even though the situation may be uncertain or dangerous.</td></tr>
<tr><td>disbelieving</td><td>ADJECTIVE If someone is or looks disbelieving, they do not believe what they are being told.</td></tr>
<tr><td>enraged</td><td>ADJECTIVE If someone is enraged, they are extremely angry.</td></tr>
<tr><td>grief-stricken</td><td>ADJECTIVE If someone is grief-stricken, they are extremely sad about something that has happened.</td></tr>
<tr><td>homesick</td><td>ADJECTIVE If you are homesick, you feel unhappy because you are away from home and are missing your family, friends, and home very much.</td></tr>
<tr><td>hysterical</td><td>1 ADJECTIVE Someone who is hysterical is in a state of uncontrolled excitement, anger, or panic.
2 ADJECTIVE Hysterical laughter is loud and uncontrolled.</td></tr>
<tr><td>idiotic</td><td>ADJECTIVE If you call someone or something idiotic, you mean that they are very stupid or silly.</td></tr>
<tr><td>indifferent</td><td>ADJECTIVE If you accuse someone of being indifferent to something, you mean that they have a complete lack of interest in it.</td></tr>
<tr><td>lovesick</td><td>ADJECTIVE If you describe someone as lovesick, you mean that they are so in love with someone that they are behaving in a strange and foolish way.</td></tr>
</table>

meditative	ADJECTIVE **Meditative** describes things that are related to the act of meditating or the act of thinking very deeply about something.	
mischievous	ADJECTIVE A **mischievous** person likes to have fun by playing harmless tricks on people or doing things they are not supposed to do.	
nasty	ADJECTIVE If you describe a person or their behaviour as **nasty**, you mean that they behave in an unkind and unpleasant way.	
revengeful	ADJECTIVE If someone is **revengeful**, they want to hurt or punish someone who has hurt or harmed them.	
self-assured	ADJECTIVE Someone who is **self-assured** shows confidence in what they say and do because they are sure of their own abilities.	
sheepish	ADJECTIVE If you look **sheepish**, you look slightly embarrassed because you feel foolish or you have done something silly.	
smug	ADJECTIVE If you say that someone is **smug**, you are criticizing the fact they seem very pleased with how good, clever, or lucky they are.	
threatened	ADJECTIVE If you feel **threatened**, you feel as if someone is trying to harm you.	
trapped	ADJECTIVE If you feel **trapped**, you are in an unpleasant situation in which you lack freedom, and you feel you cannot escape from it.	

Word Finder

Exercise 1

Complete the sentences by writing one word in each gap.

| threatened | mischievous | lovesick | self-assured | grief-stricken | sheepish |

1 People who play practical jokes are usually credited with having a _____ sense of humour.

2 The widower was _____ at the sudden loss of the wife he adored.

3 Jack gave a _____ grin and wished the earth would open up and swallow him to hide his embarrassment.

4 The district where I live is often described as dangerous, but I've never had any reason to feel _____ .

5 Despite being in her thirties, Lily felt like a _____ teenager, so strong were her feelings for Danny, who continued to ignore her.

6 James's experience of making speeches at school has made him _____ as a political speaker.

Exercise 2

Choose the correct word.

1 He couldn't escape from the situation and felt completely **mischievous / trapped / meditative**.

2 She was totally **indifferent / threatened / revengeful** and really didn't care what happened next.

3 Yes, it's exciting, children, but you need to control yourselves! I've never seen you so **enraged / hysterical / complacent** before! Calm down!

4 I'm not sure I like him but he's told me he wants to marry me, he's completely **lovesick / threatened / homesick** and carries my photo in his pocket!

5 It was awful! I've never seen her so upset! She was crying and totally **nasty / self-assured / grief-stricken**.

Exercise 3

Rearrange the letters to find words. Use the definitions to help you.

1 sebidliviegn _____ (you don't think that something is true)

2 issepehh _____ (you are a bit embarrassed because you feel you've done something stupid)

3 ffniidreetn _____ (you have no interest in something, you don't care)

4 dimevietat _____ (you often think very deeply about things)

5 ttiber _____ (you continue to feel disappointed and angry for a very long time)

6 gelufenerv _____ (you want to hurt someone because they have hurt you)

Exercise 4

Are the highlighted words correct or incorrect in the sentences?

1 It was a perfect, happy, **blissful** ❑ situation.

2 I've never been so angry! I'm absolutely **mischievous!** ❑ Completely furious!

3 I don't like him because he's so **smug** ❑, so pleased about how clever he is.

4 She was so nervous, frightened and **self-assured** ❑ that I felt sorry for her.

5 I'm not surprised you're looking **sheepish** ❑, because it was a very stupid and embarrassing thing that you did.

6 He's one of the most pleasant, confident, sociable and **nasty** ❑ people I know; I really love him.

Exercise 5

Which sentences are correct?

1 Andrei felt rather complacent about his ability to pass every exam he took. ❑

2 Jasna was often absolutely disbelieving by her brothers when they were children. ❑

3 The brothers became totally engrossed in their fight to take over the family business, and indifferent to nothing else. ❑

4 Sasha continued to feel very bitter at not being offered the job. ❑

5 They felt completely trapped by the situation and saw the perfect way out. ❑

6 The two men ahead of Emilia seemed very threatened, and she was afraid they were going to be attacked. ❑

8

Education

> **Maria** You've got a big family, haven't you, Mark? Where are all your brothers and sisters now?
>
> **Mark** Well, my elder brother got a **grant** to carry on studying, and he's completing his **master's** at the **Faculty** of Music. He's about to **submit** the **first draft** of his dissertation. He's quite **intellectual**! He got married a few years ago, as you know, and his daughter's now at **nursery** – or **kindergarten**, as some people call it.
>
> **Maria** Wow! That's amazing! And your younger brother's done well, too, I hear.
>
> **Mark** Yeah – despite the fact that he used to **skip classes** all the time, he's got a **scholarship** to go to a very posh university, which is brilliant! I gave him a hand with his **personal statement**, showed him how to use a **mind map** and so on. He's got to choose his study **options** quite soon, and get ready to move into his **hall of residence** where he'll be living. And I've just had an article published in a prestigious **journal**. The **feedback** has been good – only one reviewer muttering about **plagiarism**, but totally without foundation! Anyway, how about you, Maria?
>
> **Maria** Well, I'm carrying on with my art course. There's a **crèche** there where I can leave my daughter. And I'm putting together a **portfolio** that I can take round to prospective employers. I'm hoping I'll get some work on the strength of it.
>
> **Mark** I'm sure you will – your work's fantastic!

Word Finder		
crèche	NOUN A **crèche** is a place where small children can be left to be looked after while their parents are doing something else.	
faculty	1 NOUN A **faculty** is a group of related departments in some universities, or the people who work in them.	
	2 NOUN A **faculty** is all the teaching staff of a university or college, or of one department.	
feedback	NOUN If you get **feedback** on your work or progress, someone tells you how well or badly you are doing, and how you could improve. If you get good **feedback**, you have worked or performed well.	
grant	NOUN A **grant** is an amount of money that a government or other institution gives to an individual or to an organization for a particular purpose such as education.	
hall of residence	NOUN **Halls of residence** are buildings with rooms or flats, usually built by universities or colleges, in which students live during term time.	
intellectual	ADJECTIVE **Intellectual** means involving a person's ability to think and to understand ideas and information.	
journal	NOUN A **journal** is a magazine, especially one that deals with a specialized subject.	
kindergarten	NOUN A **kindergarten** is an informal kind of school for very young children, where they learn things by playing.	

master's	NOUN A **master's** or **master's degree** is a university degree such as an MA or MSc, which is at a higher level than a first degree and usually takes one or two years to complete.
mind map	NOUN A **mind map** is a diagram used to organize ideas or information.
nursery	NOUN A **nursery** is a place where children who are not old enough to go to school are looked after.
option	1 NOUN An **option** is something that you can choose to do in preference to one or more alternatives. 2 NOUN An **option** is one of a number of subjects which a student can choose to study as a part of his or her course.
personal statement	NOUN A **personal statement** is a piece of writing about yourself and your interests, especially one that you send as part of your application to study at a university.
plagiarism	NOUN **Plagiarism** is the practice of using or copying someone else's idea or work and pretending that you thought of it or created it yourself.
portfolio	NOUN A **portfolio** is a set of pictures by someone, or photographs of examples of their work, which they use when entering competitions or applying for work.
scholarship	NOUN If you get a **scholarship** to a school or university, your studies are paid for by the school or university or by some other organization.
skip classes	PHRASE If you **skip classes**, you do not attend lessons at school or college that you should attend.
submit	VERB If you **submit** a proposal, report, or request to someone, you formally send it to them so that they can consider it or decide about it.
tertiary education	NOUN **Tertiary education** is education at university or college level.

Word Finder

Exercise 1

Put the correct word in each gap.

master's | feedback | journal | grant | intellectual | nursery

The mature student

I was in my 30s when I decided to do a ¹ _____ in international development.
It was tough financially, but I did get a small ² _____. The university also had a
³ _____ on site, which made juggling my role as a mum with my studies a bit easier.

The course was very demanding, and at first I was worried that the other students seemed more
⁴ _____ than me. However, I had some really positive ⁵ _____ from my tutors,
which helped my confidence enormously. In fact, one of them suggested that I could adapt one of my
essays and submit it to a ⁶ _____, so I guess I must have been doing something right!

Exercise 2

Rearrange the letters to find words. Use the definitions to help you.

1 tlucyaf _____ (a group of related departments in a university)

2 roulanj _____ (a magazine about a specialized subject)

3 agreikdennrt _____ (a school for very young children)

4 fooptriol _____ (collected examples of a student's work)

5 eèrcch _____ (a place where small children are looked after while their parents work or study)

6 abcdefke _____ (comments about your work with suggestions for improvement)

Exercise 3

Which sentences are correct?

1 I went to Birmingham to study my master's degree. ❑

2 I subscribe to the journal *Nature*. ❑

3 He captured a scholarship to study at the academy. ❑

4 I decided to take the translation option in my final year. ❑

5 He asked his tutor to assign him some feedback on his work. ❑

6 She was found guilty of plagiarism and stripped of her degree. ❑

Exercise 4

Choose the correct word.

1 For your university application, you will need to write a personal **declaration / statement / announcement.**

2 She has been **skipping / jumping / omitting** classes to spend time with her boyfriend.

3 In the first year of uni, he lived in a **room / house / hall** of residence.

4 I asked my tutor to read the first **attempt / draft / script** of my dissertation.

5 When I'm planning an essay, I find it useful to make mind **maps / webs / rings**.

6 I have to **offer / propose / submit** my dissertation by the end of June.

Exercise 5

Match the sentence halves.

1 At the end of this term I have to choose

2 I asked my mum to help me write

3 When I go for the interview, I have to take

4 My parents encouraged me to apply for

5 The course I am doing is within

6 In my first year I will be living in

a the faculty of education.

b my personal statement for my university application.

c my options for the final year exams.

d a portfolio of my recent work.

e a scholarship to go to ballet school.

f one of the university's halls of residence.

9

Communication

So I **give you my word** that I will do my best to fight to lower taxes. And I'm sure I **speak on behalf of all of** you when I say we're sick and tired of tax rises and we're struggling. Just to **illustrate** my point, there have been half a dozen rises in the last year alone. To **quote** my hero James Arbuthnot, "**In short**, we've had enough." So let's just **settle the argument** of fair contributions once and for all and **assert** ourselves … Enough of the political **jargon!** We need to be heard, loud and clear, and to **make** ourselves **understood**. You all know what I'm **getting at** – we want action, and we want it now! That's strictly **off the record**, of course … .

Look at the following phrases using different verbs that appear in the exercises.

give	someone your word
make	yourself understood
put / set	the record straight
put / keep	someone in the picture
raise	your voice
settle	an argument
speak	for / on behalf of someone
take	issue with
take	someone's word for it

Good to know!

It's useful to keep a record of expressions in this way when you are trying to learn them. It will help you to clearly see which verb to use with which phrase.

assert	VERB If someone **asserts** a fact or belief, they state it firmly.
broken English	PHRASE If someone talks in **broken English**, they speak slowly and make a lot of mistakes because they do not know English very well.
demonstrate	1 VERB To **demonstrate** a fact means to make it clear to people. 2 VERB If you **demonstrate** a particular skill, quality, or feeling, you show by your actions that you have it.
get at	PHRASAL VERB If someone is **getting at** something, they are trying to express it, usually in a way that is not direct.
give your word	PHRASE If you **give** someone **your word**, you make a sincere promise to them.

Word Finder

illustrate	VERB If you use an example, story, or diagram to **illustrate** a point, you use it to show that what you are saying is true or to make your meaning clearer.
in short	PHRASE You use **in short** when you have been giving a lot of details and you want to give a conclusion or summary.
interactive	ADJECTIVE An **interactive** computer program or television system is one which allows direct communication between the user and the machine.
interpret	VERB If you **interpret** something in a particular way, you decide that this is its meaning or significance.
jargon	NOUN You use **jargon** to refer to words and expressions that are used in special or technical ways by particular groups of people, often making the language difficult to understand.
make yourself understood	PHRASE If you **make** yourself **understood**, you succeed in expressing what you mean in a way that other people can understand.
off the record	PHRASE If something that you say is **off the record**, you do not intend it to be considered as official, or published with your name attached to it.
put/keep someone in the picture	PHRASE If you **put** or **keep** someone **in the picture**, you tell them about a situation that they need to know about.
put/set the record straight	PHRASE If you **put the record straight** or **set the record straight**, you show that something that has been regarded as true is in fact not true.
quote	1 VERB If you **quote** someone, you repeat what they have written or said. 2 VERB If you **quote** something such as a law or a fact, you state it because it supports what you are saying. 3 NOUN A **quote** from a book, poem, play, or speech is a passage or phrase from it.
raise your voice	VERB If you **raise your voice**, you speak more loudly, usually because you are angry.
speak for/on behalf of someone	PHRASE If you **speak for** or **speak on behalf of** someone, you make a statement for them as their representative.
settle	VERB If people **settle** an argument or problem, or if something settles it, they solve it, for example by making a decision about who is right or about what to do.
take issue with something	PHRASE If you **take issue with** something, you disagree with it.
take someone's word for it	PHRASE If you say that you will **take** someone's **word for it**, you mean that you will accept what they say as true.

Word Finder

Exercise 1

Match the sentence halves.

1	He asserted	a	his talk with numerous examples.
2	He illustrated	b	the record straight as soon as he heard about our problem.
3	He interpreted	c	a number of authorities to support his theory.
4	He quoted	d	my remarks as personal criticism.
5	He settled	e	the matter by referring to your survey.
6	He set	f	he had no idea what was going on.

Exercise 2

Choose the correct word.

Report on progress of trainees at the London office

Overall, the latest group of trainees have progressed satisfactorily, with one possible exception. They have all [1]**demonstrated / expressed / employed** an ability to work as members of a team. One trainee (JW) has had problems [2]**getting / making / having** herself understood at times owing to her unfamilarity with some technical [3]**elocution / wording / jargon**, having previously been working in a different field. However, she is quick to understand what her trainers are [4]**getting / going / heading** at, so we do not anticipate long-term difficulties. However, in the case of NJ, it may be that he is not the right person for our organization. Two trainers have felt he was not serious about his work. I have spoken to him, for the time being off the [5]**account / record / report**, and he has given me his [6]**promise / oath / word** that he is absolutely committed to his place here, so I am going to wait until the training is over before making any further comments.

There are no other matters to mention at present.

Exercise 3

Decide if the pairs of sentences have the same meaning, as shown.

1 A In broken English, he attempted to explain his predicament.
   B He told us about his difficult situation in fluent but heavily accented English. ☒

2 A I'm suffering from a temporary deficiency in the financial department. In short, I can't pay you.
   B I'm rather short of money just now. To be honest, I can barely pay what I owe. ☐

3 A Does your company use interactive video conferencing?
   B Does your company show you video recordings of conference proceedings? ☐

4 A Do you have no one to present your side of the story to the court? ☐
   B Is there no one to speak for you when your case comes to court?

Exercise 4

Find the wrong or extra word in each sentence, as shown.

1 When we asked what he was doing, he asserted ~~it~~ that he was carrying out a survey of shoppers' preferences.

2 The guide spoke only broken up Spanish, which made it difficult for the South Americans to understand what was going on.

3 I don't speak very good Farsi, but I can generally make myself be understood.

4 Can you put down the record straight about what really occurred on the night of the 25th?

5 I have to take an issue with you over your remarks concerning his remuneration package.

6 You can take my true word for it, no one by the name of Fitzwarren has ever worked for us.

10

Words that are used together (collocations)

Collocations are words that fit together to make new phrases.

For example, a minimal number of staff on duty during a public holiday could be described as **skeleton staff**, but not ~~thin staff~~.

Tables can be effective in helping you remember different collocations. Look at the different verb + noun combinations below, which appear in the exercises in this unit.

claim	the life of someone
come	to light to terms with something under attack
get	to grips with something
pay	your respects
relish	an idea

Now look at some adjective + noun combinations that you can use.

a brisk	walk
an extinct	volcano
a feeble	attempt
a formidable	opponent
the genuine	article
in great	detail
a leisurely	walk
a lengthy	meeting
personal	effects
a vivid	description

Word Finder		
	brisk	ADJECTIVE A **brisk** walk is a quick and energetic walk.
	claim the life of	PHRASE If something such as a war or accident **claims** someone's **life**, they are killed by it.
	come to light	PHRASE If a fact **comes to light**, it becomes obvious or becomes known.
	come to terms with	PHRASE If you **come to terms with** something, you learn to accept and deal with it.
	come under attack	PHRASE If a place **comes under attack**, it starts to be attacked.
	death toll	NOUN The **death toll** of an accident, disaster, or war is the number of people who die in it.
	extinct	ADJECTIVE An **extinct** volcano is one that no longer erupts.

feeble	ADJECTIVE A **feeble** attempt to do something is not very good or likely to succeed.
formidable	ADJECTIVE Someone who is **formidable** is very great or impressive, and likely to be difficult to defeat.
genuine article	PHRASE If you say that something or someone is **the genuine article**, you mean that they are a real example of something and not false or an imitation.
get to grips with	PHRASE If you **get to grips with** something such as a problem, you start to deal with it or understand it.
leisurely	ADJECTIVE A **leisurely** walk is a slow and relaxed walk.
lengthy	ADJECTIVE A **lengthy** event or process lasts for a long time.
pay your respects	PHRASE If you **pay** your **respects** to someone, you go to see them or speak to them in order to show politeness.
personal effects	NOUN Your **personal effects** are things that belong to you and that you have or carry with you at a particular time.
relish	VERB If you **relish** something such as an idea or opportunity, you like, enjoy, or look forward to it very much.
skeleton staff	NOUN A **skeleton staff** is the smallest number of staff necessary in order to run an organization or service.
track record	NOUN If you talk about the **track record** of a person, company, or product, you are referring to their past performance, achievements, or failures in it.
vivid	ADJECTIVE A **vivid** description is very clear and detailed.

Exercise 1

Put the correct word in each gap.

> volcano | article | toll | walk | attempt | record |
> idea | staff | detail

1 a brisk _____

2 the genuine _____

3 in great _____

4 a skeleton _____

5 a track _____

6 a feeble _____

Exercise 2

Find the wrong or extra word in each sentence.

1 Unless the government gets down to grips with inflation in the very near future, they'll soon be completely out of favour with the electorate.

2 The true causes of the resignation of the entire committee became clear when certain irregularities in the accounts came to day light.

3 Joseph really relished in the idea of going to the fancy dress party disguised as an extra-terrestrial.

4 A large number of well-wishers waited patiently to pay their due respects at the memorial to those killed in the two world wars.

5 It can be very hard to come to favourable terms with being made redundant with little or no notice.

6 The sinking of the fishing vessel claimed for the lives of two members of the crew.

Exercise 3

Are the highlighted words correct or incorrect in the sentences?

1 The boxer looked the **genuine article** ❑, but his looks belied him.

2 Colin visited the cemetery to **pay his respect** ❑ to the grandfather he had never known.

3 I **revelled the idea** ❑ of spending the next six months trekking across Africa.

4 During the night the factory operated with just **skeleton employees** ❑.

5 As we approached the hive, we **went under attack** ❑ from a swarm of infuriated bees.

6 The presidential candidate faced a **formidable opponent** ❑ in the shape of the extremely popular leader of the opposition.

Exercise 4

Complete the sentences by writing one phrase in each gap.

| great detail | lengthy meeting | feeble attempt | vivid description |
| genuine article | death toll | personal effects | |

1 Gordon gave me a _____ of the woman he was to marry.

2 My aunt went into _____ about all her many ailments.

3 When the artist passed away at the height of his popularity, collectors competed to buy his _____ .

4 It was a _____ but one in which not a single decision was reached.

5 One of the paintings was clearly a poor imitation by a student, the other was the _____ – a hitherto unknown masterpiece.

6 Despite the severity of the earthquake, the _____ was less than a dozen.

Exercise 5

Complete the sentences by writing one word or phrase in each gap.

1 The doctor went into far _____ detail about the disease than I could bear.

2 Not _____ respects when her uncle had died, Carla now took the opportunity to do so.

3 Harriet was offered the post as she was the candidate with by far the strongest track _____ in marketing.

4 It was many years before Misha fully came _____ with his ignominious expulsion from school.

5 So many people had gone down with flu that the office was being run by a skeleton _____.

6 Scientists do not agree with the common misconception that volcanoes that have not erupted in recorded history are _____ .

Exercise 6

Decide if the pairs of sentences have the same meaning.

1 **A** The death toll in the epidemic reached over 5,000.
  B Over 5,000 people died in the epidemic. ❑

2 **A** The Roman army came under attack from a Celtic tribe as it crossed the river.
  B The Roman army crossed the river in order to attack a Celtic tribe. ❑

3 **A** Larry's jokes were a feeble attempt to make us all laugh.
  B We all found Larry's jokes entertaining. ❑

4 **A** I had a lengthy meeting with my solicitor about the status of my late mother's will.
  B My solicitor and I spent a long time discussing the status of my late mother's will. ❑

5 **A** The actor's personal effects were shared among his closest friends.
  B The actor had a great effect on all his closest friends. ❑

11

Phrases with *do, get* and *make*

There are a number of collocations in English that use different verbs such as **do**, **get** and **make**, where the verb itself carries no real meaning. These verbs used in this way are sometimes also called *empty verbs*, because the meaning often comes from the second part of the collocation, or the context.

Lee	Phew! We **made it**! The restaurant's still serving.
Clara	Well, what did you expect? You **did 100 mph** along the motorway! **It won't do**, Lee. One day, you'll be in trouble.
Lee	What?? I don't **get it** – you said this place **did good food**, so I **did my utmost** to get us here.
Clara	Yeah, I know... Sorry, Lee. Let's **make peace** before we go in. Anyway, you'll no doubt **make a fantastic racing driver** one day. The food here reminds me of when we **did India last year**. Come on, let's eat. I'm starving!

Look at some of the combinations with **do** and **make** that you will meet in this unit.

Verbs	Phrases
do	away with
	time (in prison)
	your utmost
make	a note of
	a point of
	an exception
	ends meet
	peace
	time to, time for
	war on
	yourself at home
	yourself understood

do away with	PHRASAL VERB To **do away with** something means to remove or get rid of it completely. To **do away with** someone means to kill them.
do time	PHRASE If someone **does time**, they spend time in prison for a crime they have committed.
do your utmost	PHRASE If you **do** your **utmost**, you try as hard as you can to do something.
get it	PHRASE If you **get** something that is said, you understand it.
make yourself at home	PHRASE If you **make** yourself **at home**, you behave in an informal, relaxed way because you feel comfortable and welcome in a place.

Word Finder

make ends meet	PHRASE If you **make ends meet**, you manage to make just enough money for the things that you really need, but no more.	
make an exception	PHRASE If you **make an exception**, you allow someone or something not to be included in a general statement, judgment, or rule.	
make it	PHRASE If you **make it** somewhere, you manage to arrive there in time for what you want to do.	
make a note of something	PHRASE If you **make a note of** something, you write it down somewhere so that you will remember it.	
make peace	PHRASE If you **make peace** with someone, you agree to stop arguing or fighting with them.	
make a point of doing something	PHRASE If you **make a point of** doing something, you do it in a very deliberate or obvious way.	
make time	PHRASE If you **make time** for something or **make time** to do something, you arrange to have some free time so that you can do it.	
make war on	PHRASE If you **make war on** someone or something that you are opposed to, you do things to stop them succeeding.	
it/that won't do	PHRASE If you say that something **won't do**, you mean that it is not good enough or not acceptable.	

Word Finder

Exercise 1

Choose the correct word.

1 I had to speak very slowly just to **make / get** myself understood.

2 I've **done / made** a note of all the jobs that need doing.

3 Come in! Sit down and **make / get** yourself at home.

4 Luis was **making / doing** his utmost to appear cheerful, but I guessed he was feeling pretty anxious.

5 These cars can **do / make** 120 miles per hour without any difficulty.

6 Like everyone else, I'm busy, but I try to **make / do** time to see my friends.

Exercise 2

Match the two parts.

1 Most restaurants won't take on new staff for such short periods of time.

2 How about Café Pisa for lunch?

3 So how many pounds is twenty-nine kilos?

4 Marina is really good at explaining things.

5 Does the work need to be done right now?

6 And Kurt has two jobs, does he?

a You've got me there!

b No, next week will do.

c Yes, just to make ends meet.

d Is that the place where they do really good pizzas?

e She'd make a good teacher.

f Perhaps they'll make an exception for you.

Exercise 3

For each question, tick the correct answer.

1 If you make ends meet, do you
❑ hold hands with someone?
❑ have just enough money to pay for the necessities of life?
❑ succeed in communicating with someone?

2 If someone does away with something, do they
❑ abolish or get rid of something?
❑ put something in a cupboard?
❑ lose something?

3 If you say that someone makes it, do you mean they
❑ pretend to be something they are not?
❑ succeed in a particular activity or career in which most people fail, for example acting?
❑ laugh very loudly?

4 If someone does time, do they
❑ wait for someone?
❑ do something very slowly?
❑ spend a period in prison?

5 If someone does their utmost, do they
❑ try extremely hard to do something?
❑ die?
❑ stretch their arm in order to reach something?

Exercise 4

Which sentences are correct?

1 I don't usually break for coffee when I'm working but I'll do an exception for you.   ❑

2 The government has called on the two sides to make peace.   ❑

3 We must continue the fight against those who make war on society.   ❑

4 Sara does a point of using people's names when she's speaking to them.   ❑

5 I hope you did a note of your password.   ❑

6 We helped ourselves to food and drinks and generally made ourselves at home.   ❑

Exercise 5

Are the highlighted words correct or incorrect in this text?

Spain was fabulous – Seville and Huelva the highlights of our trip (we thought we'd **do** ❑ both cities while we were in the south). Andrew seemed to know all about every church and castle that we visited – he'd **do** ❑ a good tour guide! Sadly, my Spanish is fairly poor and I had some difficulty **making** ❑ myself understood. Andrew, meanwhile, **did** ❑ a point of ordering in perfect Spanish everywhere we went. If you ever visit either city, btw, I've **done** ❑ a note of two restaurants in particular that **do** ❑ the best paella.

12

Health, medicine and exercise

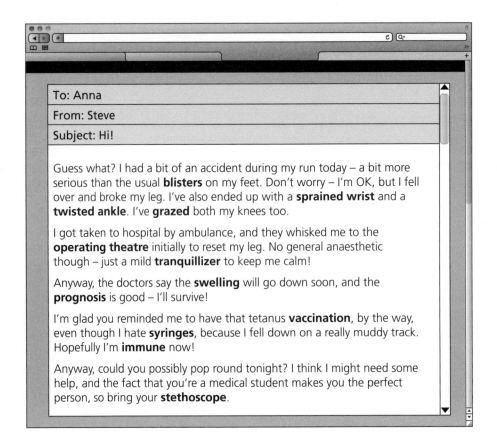

Meadow Lane Health Centre

CONFIDENTIAL

Patient's name: John Jones

Doctor's name: Dr R Patel

Patient's symptoms: Feels **nauseous**, complaining of stomach **cramps**

Diagnosis: Query food poisoning?

Treatment: Prescribed antibiotics, **dosage** two tablets to be taken twice a day, **blood sample** sent for analysis

NB Mr Jones is **allergic to** penicillin

To: Anna
From: Steve
Subject: Hi!

Guess what? I had a bit of an accident during my run today – a bit more serious than the usual **blisters** on my feet. Don't worry – I'm OK, but I fell over and broke my leg. I've also ended up with a **sprained wrist** and a **twisted ankle**. I've **grazed** both my knees too.

I got taken to hospital by ambulance, and they whisked me to the **operating theatre** initially to reset my leg. No general anaesthetic though – just a mild **tranquillizer** to keep me calm!

Anyway, the doctors say the **swelling** will go down soon, and the **prognosis** is good – I'll survive!

I'm glad you reminded me to have that tetanus **vaccination**, by the way, even though I hate **syringes**, because I fell down on a really muddy track. Hopefully I'm **immune** now!

Anyway, could you possibly pop round tonight? I think I might need some help, and the fact that you're a medical student makes you the perfect person, so bring your **stethoscope**.

allergic	ADJECTIVE If you are **allergic** to something, you become ill or get a rash when you eat it, smell it, or touch it.
blister	NOUN A **blister** is a painful swelling on the surface of your skin. **Blisters** contain a clear liquid and are usually caused by heat or by something repeatedly rubbing your skin.
blood sample	NOUN A **blood sample** is a small amount of someone's blood that can be tested to see if it contains a particular substance or if the person has a medical condition.
cramp	NOUN **Cramp** is a sudden strong pain caused by a muscle suddenly contracting. You sometimes get **cramp** in a muscle after you have been making a physical effort over a long period of time.
diagnosis	NOUN **Diagnosis** is the discovery and naming of what is wrong with someone who is ill or with something that is not working properly.
dosage	NOUN A **dosage** is the amount of a medicine or drug that someone takes or should take.
epidemic	NOUN If there is an **epidemic** of a particular disease somewhere, it affects a very large number of people there and spreads quickly to other areas.
graze	1 VERB If you **graze** a part of your body, you injure your skin by scraping against something. 2 NOUN A **graze** is a small wound caused by scraping against something.
immune	ADJECTIVE If you are **immune** to a particular disease, you cannot be affected by it.
immune system	NOUN Your **immune system** consists of all the organs and processes in your body which protect you from illness and infection.
nauseous	ADJECTIVE If you feel **nauseous**, you feel as if you want to vomit.
operating theatre	NOUN An **operating theatre** is a special room in a hospital where surgeons carry out medical operations.
preventative medicine	NOUN **Preventative medicine** consists of treatments and actions that are intended to help prevent people becoming ill.
prognosis	NOUN A **prognosis** is an estimate of the future of someone or something, especially about whether a patient will recover from an illness.
sprained	ADJECTIVE A **sprained** ankle or wrist is one that has been damaged by being twisted or bent violently.
stethoscope	NOUN A **stethoscope** is an instrument that a doctor uses to listen to your heart and breathing. It consists of a small disc that is placed on your body, connected to a hollow tube with two pieces that the doctor puts in his or her ears.
swelling	NOUN A **swelling** is a raised, curved shape on the surface of your body which appears as a result of an injury or an illness.

Word Finder

syringe	NOUN A **syringe** is a small tube with a thin hollow needle at the end. **Syringes** are used for putting liquids into things and for taking liquids out, for example for injecting drugs or for taking blood from someone's body.
tranquillizer	NOUN A **tranquillizer** is a drug that makes someone calm, sleepy, or unconscious.
twisted	ADJECTIVE A **twisted** ankle or wrist has been injured by being turned too sharply.
vaccination	NOUN A **vaccination** is a substance containing a harmless form of the germs that cause a particular disease, put into someone's body to stop them from getting the disease, usually by an injection.

Word Finder

Exercise 1

Complete the sentences by writing one word or phrase in each gap.

> dosages | twisted ankles | cramps | blood samples | syringes |
> epidemics | blisters

1 My new boots rubbed so badly that I had a couple of large _____ on my feet by the end of the walk.

2 Tina woke up in the middle of the night with worse stomach _____ than she had ever experienced before.

3 The hospital changed its supplier of _____ because so many had been faulty.

4 The doctor decided to reduce the _____ of both the medicines I was taking, because of the side-effects I was suffering.

5 I've had to go to the surgery several times to give _____, and the doctor still can't work out what's causing my symptoms.

6 No smallpox _____ have occurred since the disease was declared eradicated in 1979.

Exercise 2

Choose the correct word or phrase.

1 I can't eat shellfish because I'm **immune / allergic** to it.

2 The doctor's **prognosis / diagnosis** was that she had an excellent chance of recovery.

3 I'm going to increase the **dosage / tranquillizer** of morphine so that you can manage the pain more easily.

4 I've got a **swelling / sprained** wrist from playing tennis.

5 Pierre's **immune system / blood sample** produced a negative result.

6 Tegan came back from her skiing trip with a **grazed / twisted** ankle.

Exercise 3

Put the correct word or phrase in each gap.

> dosage | prognosis | twisted | diagnosis | syringe | blood samples |
> stethoscope | operating theatre | vaccinations

12th December

Took baby to the doctor's today for her [1] _____. She screamed when she saw the [2] _____! She must have guessed it was going to hurt her. He also listened to her chest but the [3] _____ must have been cold as she started screaming again! I was glad to get home.

Mum will be in the [4] _____ this time tomorrow. I'm not too worried because the [5] _____ is good so she should soon be on the mend.

Leo's [6] _____ his ankle playing football, so I may need to take him for an X-ray tomorrow. Hopefully that will be the end of all these medical visits for a while!

Exercise 4

Rearrange the letters to find words. Use the definitions to help you.

1 essouaun _____ (a feeling of wanting to vomit)

2 muniem _____ (referring to the system that protects the body against disease)

3 llingswe _____ (an enlargement of part of the body due to accumulating liquid)

4 reltnraqlizui _____ (a medicine which helps to reduce anxiety)

5 medipeci _____ (a widespread occurrence of an infectious disease, such as flu)

6 rpmca _____ (a painful muscle contraction)

Exercise 5

Which sentences are correct?

1 Katya grazed her knee and had to put a plaster on it. ❏

2 The diagnosis is great – he should be fully recovered in a month or two. ❏

3 The idea behind preventative medicine is that you shouldn't become sick with what you're being protected against. ❏

4 Twists and sprains are pretty much the same thing. ❏

5 If you're allergic to something you are immune to it. ❏

6 Jen felt quite nauseous during the first three months of her pregnancy. ❏

13

Entertainment and the media

TV Guide

20.30	Grab the Gold	**Contestants** compete to win the top prize – now at £1million!
21.00	Artnews	Reviewers discuss the entrants in this year's Perry Award for Art. Favourites include the **illustrations** of Chris Grey, and the **sketches** of Anna Ferris. Also **playwright** John Malcolm talks about his new play, 'The View from the Theatre **Stalls**', performed in Chinese with **subtitles**.
21.00	Film: Where There's Hope	Brilliant thriller **shot** in Rome – **dubbed** into English. Look out for a young Maya James as an **extra** in one of the street scenes!
23.00	News Extra	In-depth current affairs discussion programme. This week: What does the future hold for the **tabloid press** and the kind of stories they **run**? Are the **paparazzi** beginning to go too far? Which academic **journals** are the most prestigious now – and why? Ring in while the programme is **on air**. **Transmitted** again at 01.00.
23.50	Music Now	The latest in **techno** music. Well-known musicians **cover** the hits – live in the studio!

Word Finder

contestant	NOUN A **contestant** in a competition or quiz is a person who takes part in it.
cover	VERB To **cover** a song originally performed by someone else means to record a new version of it.
dubbed	ADJECTIVE If a film is **dubbed**, a new soundtrack is added by actors speaking a different language from the one used originally.
extra	NOUN An **extra** in a film is someone who plays an unimportant part, for example, as a member of a crowd.
gig	NOUN A **gig** is a live performance by someone such as a musician or comedian.
illustration	NOUN An **illustration** in a book is a picture, design, or diagram.
index	NOUN An **index** is an alphabetical list that is printed at the back of a book and tells you on which pages important topics are referred to.
journal	1 NOUN A **journal** is a magazine, especially one that deals with a specialized subject. 2 NOUN A **journal** is a daily or weekly newspaper. The word **journal** is often used in the name of the paper.
on air	ADJECTIVE If a programme is **on air**, it is being broadcast on radio or television.
paparazzi	NOUN The **paparazzi** are photographers who follow famous people around, hoping to take interesting or shocking photographs that they can sell to a newspaper.
playwright	NOUN A **playwright** is a person who writes plays.

Word Finder		
run	VERB If newspapers or magazines **run** a particular item or story or if it **runs**, it is published or printed.
shoot	VERB When people **shoot** a film or **shoot** photographs, they make a film or take photographs using a camera.
sketch	NOUN A **sketch** is a drawing that is done quickly without a lot of details. Artists often use **sketches** as a preparation for a more detailed painting or drawing.
stalls	NOUN The **stalls** in a theatre are the seats on the ground floor, directly in front of the stage.
subtitles	NOUN If a film or TV programme has **subtitles**, the words that are being spoken are written across the bottom of the screen, sometimes translated into a different language.
tabloid press	NOUN The **tabloid press** consists of the most popular and least serious newspapers, usually with small pages and a lot of pictures and stories about famous people.
techno	NOUN **Techno** is a form of modern electronic music with a very fast beat.
telly	NOUN A **telly** is a television.
transmit	VERB When radio and television programmes, computer data, or other electronic messages are **transmitted**, they are sent from one place to another, using wires, radio waves, or satellites.

Exercise 1

Put the correct word in each gap.

stalls | gigs | paparazzi | sketches | contestants | illustrations | playwrights | extras

1 people who take part in quizzes or competitions: _____

2 pictures or diagrams, drawn by artists, for books: _____

3 photographers who follow celebrities in order to take pictures: _____

4 drawings which are done quickly, often as preparation for paintings or sculptures: _____

5 seats on the ground floor in a theatre, near the stage: _____

6 live performances by people such as musicians or comedians: _____

Exercise 2

Rearrange the letters to find words. Use the definitions to help you.

1 uselsbtti _____ (a printed translation of the words of a foreign film that are shown at the bottom of the picture)

2 ctenoh _____ (a form of modern electronic music with a very fast beat)

3 najurol _____ (a magazine specializing in a particular, often academic, subject)

4 wpylagthir _____ (a person who writes plays)

5 xedin _____ (an alphabetical list that is printed at the back of a book and tells you the pages on which important topics are referred to)

6 vcero _____ (to record a song which has already been written and recorded by another artist)

Exercise 3

Choose the correct word.

1 Important football matches are usually **run / shot / transmitted** live around the world so that fans can see the action as it happens.

2 Radio shows aren't usually pre-recorded, so if the host makes a mistake on **telly / air / sketch** then all the listeners hear it.

3 300,000 **extras / paparazzi / playwrights** were used in the enormous crowd scenes in the film *Gandhi*.

4 Leonardo da Vinci made hundreds of quick **subtitles / sketches / covers** of human anatomy to understand the human body better.

5 The film was very badly **run / covered / dubbed** – a lot of the jokes were left out.

Exercise 4

Match the sentence halves.

1 Have you ever wanted to be a game-show   a press for invading their privacy.

2 The size of a print   b run depends on the number of books that will sell.

3 Celebrities often criticize the tabloid   c extras to earn a bit of money while they are waiting for their 'big break'.

4 The USA was the birthplace of techno   d contestant and win lots of money?

5 Artists who specialize in children's book   e music during the mid 1980s.

6 Out-of-work actors often work as film   f illustration often become famous.

Exercise 5

Put the correct word in each gap.

| playwright | subtitles | stalls | extras | telly | paparazzi | shoot |

When the famous [1] _____ William Shakespeare put quill to parchment in the 16th century, it's unlikely that he could ever have imagined the variety of forms his plays would take over the years. Movie versions can certainly make the plays seem more relevant to contemporary audiences. For example, the director Baz Luhrmann made the decision to [2] _____ *Romeo and Juliet* in Mexico and Florida and to set it in the present day. He also cast glamorous Hollywood actors, more used to being photographed by the [3] _____ than to speaking 16th century English. As well as films, many of Shakespeare's plays have been adapted for [4] _____, some with considerable success. There's no doubt that the battle scenes are more realistic because of the thousands of [5] _____ who are hired to take part. Of course, it's still possible to enjoy a Shakespeare play from the [6] _____ of many theatres. Traditionalists might prefer to visit the Globe theatre in London, which is a reconstruction of the original theatre for which Shakespeare wrote plays in the 16th century.

14

People – character and behaviour

Character reference

CONFIDENTIAL

Name of applicant: *James Macfarlane*

Post applied for: *Team leader*

How long have you known the applicant? *5 years*

In what capacity? *As his line manager*

Please use the space below to supply information that will support his/her application:

*I have worked closely with James over the past five years, during which time he has shown himself to be a **conscientious** and **trustworthy** young man. He is an extremely **gifted** and **knowledgeable** scientist, but at the same time very **modest** about his talents. He has also proved to be extremely **supportive** of the PhD students who have worked with him. I would have no hesitation in recommending him for this post.*

Look at the table below. It shows the adjectives you will learn in the unit, and whether they convey a positive or negative meaning.

Positive	Negative
alert	anti-social
chatty	introvert
courageous	narrow-minded
extrovert	
rational	
heroic	
sincere	
stable	
talkative	

alert		ADJECTIVE If you are **alert**, you are paying full attention to things around you and are prepared to deal with anything that might happen.
anti-social		ADJECTIVE Someone who is **anti-social** is unwilling to meet and be friendly with other people.
chatty		ADJECTIVE Someone who is **chatty** talks a lot in a friendly, informal way.
conscientious		ADJECTIVE Someone who is **conscientious** is very careful to do their work properly.
courageous		ADJECTIVE Someone who is **courageous** shows courage and bravery.
devastated		ADJECTIVE If you are **devastated** by something, you are very shocked and upset by it.
extrovert		1 ADJECTIVE Someone who is **extrovert** is very active, lively, and friendly. 2 NOUN An **extrovert** is someone who is extrovert.
frustrating		ADJECTIVE Something that is **frustrating** annoys you or makes you angry because you cannot do anything about the problems it causes.
gifted		ADJECTIVE Someone who is **gifted** has a natural ability to do something well.
heroic		ADJECTIVE If you describe a person or their actions as **heroic**, you admire them because they show extreme bravery.
introvert		NOUN An **introvert** is a quiet, shy person who finds it difficult to talk to people.
knowledgeable		ADJECTIVE Someone who is **knowledgeable** has or shows a clear understanding of many different facts about the world or about a particular subject.
modest		ADJECTIVE If you say that someone is **modest**, you approve of them because they do not talk much about their abilities or achievements.
narrow-minded		ADJECTIVE If you describe someone as **narrow-minded**, you are criticizing them because they are unwilling to consider new ideas or other people's opinions.
rational		ADJECTIVE A **rational** person is someone who is sensible and is able to make decisions based on intelligent thinking rather than on emotion.
sincere		ADJECTIVE If you say that someone is **sincere**, you approve of them because they really mean the things they say. You can also describe someone's behaviour and beliefs as **sincere**.
stable		ADJECTIVE If someone has a **stable** personality, they are calm and reasonable and their mood does not change suddenly.
supportive		ADJECTIVE If you are **supportive**, you are kind and helpful to someone at a difficult or unhappy time in their life.
talkative		ADJECTIVE Someone who is **talkative** talks a lot.
trustworthy		ADJECTIVE A **trustworthy** person is reliable, responsible, and can be trusted completely.

Word Finder

Work on your Vocabulary Advanced (C1)

Exercise 1

Match the sentence halves.

1 He seemed very knowledgeable

2 He uses various strategies to stay alert

3 He was absolutely devastated

4 I think he was being sincere

5 He was modest about his achievements

6 He was extremely supportive

a when he is driving long distances.

b when I spoke to him about the history of the castle.

c when I called to congratulate him.

d when his marriage failed.

e when he said he admired my work.

f when I was having problems at work.

Exercise 2

Choose the correct word.

1 Sadly, she lost her **concerted / courageous / crushing** fight against the disease.

2 Despite his success, he remains **middling / marginal / modest** about his own work.

3 A job in sales would be perfect for her because she is such an **enthusiast / extrovert / entrepreneur.**

4 He often stays late at work because he's very **conscientious / conscious / conspicuous.**

5 Your new friend is extremely **tentative / talkative / tenuous.**

6 She seems to be incapable of **rational / residual / reciprocal** behaviour.

Exercise 3

Put the correct word in each gap.

| stable | extrovert | anti-social | gifted | frustrating | supportive |

Peter and Daisy

My brother Peter has always been a [1] _____ pianist, but he never seemed able to settle down and was always moving from job to job. However, since 2005, when he met his future wife Daisy, his life has been much more [2] _____. He and Daisy now have a lovely home in Devon, and she's very [3] _____ of his career.

I still worry about them though, because although Daisy's lovely, she's a great [4] _____. I sometimes think it must be [5] _____ for her to be married to someone like my brother, who is really terribly [6] _____ and would always rather sit at home than go out with friends.

Exercise 4

Put the synonym in each gap.

> distraught | genuine | dependable | logical | talkative | informed | talented | heroic

1 devastated _____
2 sincere _____
3 courageous _____
4 knowledgeable _____
5 gifted _____
6 chatty _____
7 rational _____
8 trustworthy _____

Exercise 5

Complete the sentences by writing one word in each gap.

> courageous | introvert | modest | frustrating | narrow-minded | trustworthy | talkative | devastated

1 She is an _____ by nature and finds the social aspects of her job very difficult.

2 He took the _____ decision to give up a well-paid job and train as an actor.

3 They are too _____ to accept that a different way of life can be just as valid as their own.

4 Although she's too _____ to admit it, she knows the company would never have succeeded without her.

5 Her inability to win a major tournament has been extremely _____ for her.

6 He needs to be sure that all his security staff are completely _____.

Exercise 6

Which sentences are correct?

1 He gave a very gifted performance of the Beethoven. ❏
2 Over the summer, there has been an increase in anti-social behaviour. ❏
3 It must be frustrating of you when nobody replies to your letters. ❏
4 He was conscientious to work hard before the exams. ❏
5 My parents were supportive to my decision to go to drama school. ❏
6 I was shocked by their narrow-minded responses to my announcement. ❏

15

Relationships

Ask Janice Advice from your favourite **agony aunt**

❤

Dear Janice,
My best friend is 29 years old and **unmarried**, and she's recently become very **attached** to a male colleague at work – a **widower**. She says she feels she can really **relate** to him and that there's a real **bond** between them. They went out a few times, but just recently he's started **giving her the cold shoulder**. I think he's been seeing someone else, and I can see real **jealousy** flaring up in her. I keep telling her to try and forget the whole thing. I don't want to **nag** her, but I do want to give her some advice – what should I say?

Yours,
Keen to Help

Dear Keen to Help,
Is it possible this man prefers to be just an **acquaintance** rather than an **item** with your friend? If he's on a **social networking site**, she could contact him that way and talk about it. Workplace relationships aren't always a good idea – in fact some offices are quite **strict** about them, so that may explain this man's behaviour.

Yours,
Janice

Dear Janice,
I come from a big **extended** family and I would love to be a **foster parent** to some children – but my partner doesn't agree. I'm in a **civil partnership**, and in the **vows** we took, we agreed to respect each other's wishes – but that hasn't happened. My **half-sister** says I should talk this through with my partner, but I feel so angry right now. What should I do?

Yours,
Resentful

Dear Resentful,
Your **half-sister** is right – you do need to talk this through, as these feelings will never go away, and you'll feel even more resentful. Don't let this come between you!

Yours,
Janice

Word Finder

acquaintance	NOUN An **acquaintance** is someone who you have met and know slightly, but not well.
agony aunt	NOUN An **agony aunt** is a person who writes a column in a newspaper or magazine in which they reply to readers who have written to them for advice on their personal problems.
attached	ADJECTIVE If you are **attached** to someone, you like them very much.
bond	NOUN A **bond** between people is a strong feeling of friendship, love, or shared beliefs and experiences that unite them.
civil partnership	NOUN A **civil partnership** is a legal relationship between two men or two women, that gives them the same rights as a married couple.

extended family	NOUN An **extended family** is a family group which includes relatives such as uncles, aunts, and grandparents, as well as parents, children, and brothers and sisters.
foster parent	NOUN **Foster parents** are people who officially take a child into their family for a period of time, without becoming the child's legal parents. The child is referred to as their foster child.
give someone the cold shoulder	PHRASE If you **give someone the cold shoulder**, you are not friendly or sympathetic to them.
half-sister	NOUN Your **half-sister** is a woman or girl who has either the same mother or the same father as you.
hospitality	NOUN **Hospitality** is friendly, welcoming behaviour towards guests or people you have just met.
item	NOUN If two people are an **item**, they are a couple who are having a romantic relationship.
jealousy	NOUN **Jealousy** is the feeling of anger or bitterness which someone has when they think that another person is trying to take a lover or friend, or a possession, away from them.
nag	VERB If someone **nags** you, they keep asking you to do something you have not done yet or do not want to do.
social networking site	NOUN A **social networking site** is a website such as Facebook, Twitter, or Tumblr where you can share information, news, and photographs with friends.
strict	ADJECTIVE If a parent or other person in authority is **strict**, they regard many actions as unacceptable and do not allow them.
unit	NOUN If you consider two people as a **unit**, you consider them together as a couple.
unmarried	ADJECTIVE Someone who is **unmarried** is not married.
vow	NOUN **Vows** are a particular set of serious promises, such as the promises two people make when they are getting married.
widower	NOUN A **widower** is a man whose wife has died and who has not married again.

Word Finder

Exercise 1

Match the sentence halves.

1 Gary's an acquaintance
2 Dermot gave Timmy
3 Maggie's my half-sister –
4 They've been an item
5 Mick's a widower –
6 I feel very attached to

a we have the same mum.
b for several months.
c he's lived alone since his wife died.
d my new boyfriend already.
e the cold shoulder.
f of mine.

Exercise 2

For each question, tick the correct answer.

1 If you form a bond with someone, you
   - ❏ make a promise to them.
   - ❏ develop a close relationship with them.

2 If you relate to someone, you
   - ❏ are part of the same family.
   - ❏ understand how they feel.

3 What do foster parents do?
   - ❏ They look after a child in place of its natural parents.
   - ❏ They commit to developing their child's natural abilities.

4 What is a civil partnership?
   - ❏ The relationship between an unmarried couple.
   - ❏ A legal union between a same-sex couple, granting rights similar to a marriage.

5 What is an agony aunt?
   - ❏ Someone who writes a magazine column, giving advice to people who write in with problems.
   - ❏ Someone who helps people manage pain caused by chronic illlness.

Exercise 3

Rearrange the letters to find words. Use the definitions to help you.

1 ttsrci _____ (making someone behave well and obey the rules)

2 ddeeentx myliaf _____ (blood relatives of three or more generations)

3 laeyoujs _____ (wanting what someone else has, or resenting them for having something you don't have yourself)

4 wvo _____ (a solemn promise or decision)

5 agn _____ (to constantly and openly criticize someone or demand things from them)

6 yttaiiohspl _____ (being friendly and welcoming to guests)

Exercise 4

Put the correct ending in each gap.

we've formed a special bond. | for no particular reason. | we don't like each other. | you're driving me mad! | is called a single parent. | a mere acquaintance. | no one will come between them.

1 They're a pretty close unit – _____

2 He's been giving me the cold shoulder _____

3 She's no more than _____

4 Stop nagging at me – _____

5 Over the years _____

6 A person raising a child on their own _____

16

Computers, mobile phones and research

Read the two emails between the lecturer and IT support:

To: Max Samuels, IT Support (**Programmer**)

From: Stella Rogers, Lecturer

Subject: IT problem

Could you spare a minute to come down and look at my computer, Max? A message has just **come up** on my screen and I'm wondering if I've picked up a virus. I've been getting a lot of **spam** emails lately – could it have been from those? Or during the **installation** of the new software?

I'm sorry to sound so **technologically** challenged – but I've got a **case study** on **genetic engineering** that I urgently need to **scan** and send to students this morning – connected with their **research findings** – so I'd be really grateful if you could come as soon as you can.

Thanks.

To: Stella Rogers, Lecturer

From: Max Samuels, IT Support (**Programmer**)

Subject: Re: IT problem

I'll come as soon as I can, but a number of computers are **down** at the moment, and I'm hoping to **experiment** with some new **gadgets** we bought to find out why. We've installed a number of security **devices** on our computers, so there shouldn't be a problem. If I can find a scanner that's **compatible** with one of the working computers, you can **scan** your document on that.

Word Finder

case study	NOUN A **case study** is a written account that gives detailed information about a person, group, or thing and their development over a period of time.
come up	PHRASAL VERB If information **comes up**, it appears, for example on a computer screen.
compatible	ADJECTIVE If one make of computer or computer equipment is **compatible** with another make, they can be used together and can use the same software.
developer	NOUN A **developer** is someone who develops something such as a piece of software, a design, or a product.
device	NOUN A **device** is an object that has been invented for a particular purpose, for example for recording or measuring something.

Word Finder

down	ADJECTIVE If a piece of equipment, especially a computer system, is **down**, it is temporarily not working because of a fault.
experiment	1 NOUN An **experiment** is a scientific test which is done in order to discover what happens to something in particular conditions.
	2 VERB If you **experiment** with something or experiment on it, you do a scientific test on it in order to discover what happens to it in particular conditions.
findings	NOUN Someone's **findings** are the information they get or the conclusions they come to as the result of an investigation or experiment.
gadget	NOUN A **gadget** is a small machine or device which does something useful.
genetic engineering	NOUN **Genetic engineering** is the science or activity of changing the genetic structure of an animal, plant, or other organism in order to make it stronger or more suitable for a particular purpose.
installation	NOUN The **installation** of software is the process of putting it onto a computer so that it is ready to use.
language	NOUN A computer **language** is a particular system of giving instructions to a computer in the form of programs.
nanotechnology	NOUN **Nanotechnology** is the science of making or working with things that are so small that they can only be seen using a powerful microscope.
programmer	NOUN A **programmer** is a person whose job involves writing programs for computers.
scan	VERB If a picture or document is **scanned** into a computer, a machine passes a beam of light over it to make a copy of it in the computer.
smart	ADJECTIVE A **smart** card or **smart** phone uses computer technology to perform more advanced functions than earlier models of the same thing. For example, a **smart** phone has many of the capabilities of a small computer, and can access the Internet.
spam	NOUN In computing, **spam** or a **spam email** is an unwanted email that is sent to a large number of people, usually as advertising.
technologically	ADVERB In a way that relates to or uses **technology** such as computers.
transmit	VERB When radio and television programmes, computer data, or other electronic messages are **transmitted**, they are sent from one place to another, using wires, radio waves, or satellites.
unfounded	ADJECTIVE If a claim or belief is **unfounded**, it is wrong because it is not based on facts or evidence.

Exercise 1

Choose the correct word.

1 A memory stick is a **device / method / design** which you can use to store documents or photographs on electronically.

2 Do you know what this message means? It has just **taken / come / brought** up on my screen.

3 Dr Paraskevas has been working on **a research / a test / an experiment** in the computer laboratory, but I don't think she is ready to share her **findings / answers / responses**.

4 That new computer technician is great. She did the **organization / setting / installation** of my new computer and printer in record time.

Exercise 2

Match the sentence halves.

1 A computer programmer usually

2 If you scan a document

3 When someone says their computer is down, it means

4 A smart credit card is one which

5 If you transmit a message, it means you

a you can use for lots of different purposes.

b knows how to develop new games for the computer.

c you make an electronic copy which you can save onto your computer.

d send it out to other receivers, e.g. by radio.

e it is not working.

Exercise 3

Are the highlighted words correct or incorrect in the sentences?

1 You should delete any **spam** ❑ you get on your computer. It is usually nothing but adverts.

2 Many science students are expected to carry out **experiments** ❑ and report their **answers.** ❑

3 When machines are so complex that they can function independently, we use the term **clever.** ❑

4 An **unfounded** ❑ claim or belief is one that is based on a lot of reading and research.

5 If you have a new computer program on your machine, you need to make sure that it is **compatible** ❑ with those of other people you will be working with.

6 I keep getting a strange message coming **on** ❑ my computer.

Exercise 4

Complete the sentences by writing one word in each gap.

1 Why don't you _____ these photos into your computer, because then you would have your own digital copies.

2 The new hard drive we bought is an incredible _____. It can store so much more than my laptop can.

3 The _____ of all the new computers in my office took several days. They had to replace our old computers and printers with new ones.

4 Emma is a computer [a] _____ who is very good at using computer [b] _____ to develop all sorts of programs and games.

5 Sometimes I have no idea what the messages that come _____ on my laptop screen actually mean. Could you please have a look at it for me?

6 Our next degree examination is based on a _____ study. They give us the details of a particular situation and we have to answer questions about it in the actual examination.

Exercise 5

Which sentences are correct?

1 Yesterday, a virus infected all our machines and our computers were up for most of the afternoon. ❑

2 These two machines are just not compatible. They won't transmit messages to each other. ❑

3 Johnny is an excellent software developer and works on very complicated computer programs. ❑

4 Gadget and device cannot be synonyms. ❑

5 Smart technology means that the machines are stylish and expensive. ❑

6 Many people believe that genetic engineering is immoral and should be stopped. ❑

Exercise 6

For each question, tick the correct answer.

1 If a claim is unfounded, it means that
  ❑ it is true and can be proved.
  ❑ it is not based on any facts.
  ❑ it is from a secret source.

2 What is nanotechnology about?
  ❑ Developing computers that can be used underwater.
  ❑ Developing tiny devices at the level of atoms.
  ❑ Developing technology that is heavy to carry.

3 If an email message is categorized as spam, you should
  ❑ forward it to a friend.
  ❑ save the contents to your computer.
  ❑ delete it immediately.

4 A case study is when
  ❑ a particular person or situation is being researched and documented.
  ❑ a court case is being filmed.
  ❑ a problem faced by passengers and airlines is identified.

5 What is genetic engineering?
  ❑ The engineering and construction of ever taller buildings in city centres.
  ❑ The use of medication for diseases that affect very young babies.
  ❑ The development of organisms by the manipulation of their genetic make-up.

17

Talking about experiences

I've always had an **aptitude** for managing people. So when the chance came to join the senior management team at my company, not long after I'd joined, I jumped at it. I was **highly ambitious**, I **excelled** at what I did, and I **fitted in** with the team immediately – I felt very **at home** in that environment. And as someone who was largely **self-taught** in terms of my **specialization**, I thought I'd done amazingly well. I loved the job, and **immersed** myself in it completely, and the **lifestyle** that went with it.

Imagine my dismay, then, when the company's fortunes took a downturn, and I was **made redundant** – last in, first out, as they told me, and that did make me feel rather an **outsider**. You can see the **impact** it would undoubtedly have on my life.

Anyway, I was at least **eligible** for some redundancy pay. I **opted for** some programmes that would help me **retrain**, and within no time at all I found another job – even better than my previous one. So the message is, if you find yourself in my position, don't give up. The **consequences** may not be as dire as you think!

ambitious	ADJECTIVE If you are **ambitious**, you have a strong desire to be successful, rich, or powerful.
aptitude	NOUN If you have an **aptitude** for something, you are naturally good at it.
consequence	NOUN The **consequences** of something are the results or effects of it.
distinction	NOUN **Distinction** is the quality of being very good or better than other things of the same type.
eligible	ADJECTIVE If you are **eligible** for something, you are qualified or able to have it.
excel	VERB If you **excel** at something, you are very good at it.
feel at home	PHRASE If you **feel at home** in a situation, you feel comfortable and relaxed in it.
fit in	PHRASAL VERB If you **fit in** with a group of people, you are happy and accepted in that group because you are similar to them.
immerse yourself	VERB If you **immerse yourself** in something, you become completely involved in it.
impact	NOUN The **impact** that something has on a situation, process, or person is a sudden and powerful effect that it has on them.
lifestyle	NOUN The **lifestyle** of a particular person or group of people is the living conditions, behaviour, and habits that are typical of them or are chosen by them.
be made redundant	PHRASE If someone **is made redundant**, they are asked to leave a company because there is no longer a job for them.
nurture	1 VERB If you **nurture** something such as a young child or a young plant, you care for it while it is growing and developing.
	2 VERB If you **nurture** plans, ideas, or people, you encourage them or help them to develop.

Word Finder

Word Finder	**opt for**	PHRASAL VERB If you **opt for** something, you choose it or decide to do it.
	outsider	NOUN An **outsider** is someone who does not belong to a particular group or organization.
	retrain	VERB If you **retrain**, you learn new skills, especially in order to get a new job.
	self-made	ADJECTIVE **Self-made** is used to describe people who have become successful and rich through their own efforts, especially if they started life without money, education, or high social status
	self-taught	ADJECTIVE If you are **self-taught**, you have learned a skill by yourself rather than being taught it by someone else.
	specialization	NOUN Your **specialization** is a particular area of your work or subject that you know a lot about.

Exercise 1

Are the highlighted words correct or incorrect in the sentences?

1 When he arrived in Cambridge, he immersed himself **in** ❑ his studies.

2 After having children, Vicki decided to retrain **for** ❑ a social worker.

3 Watching these athletes winning Olympic medals made a big impact **of** ❑ me.

4 For her degree subjects, she opted **for** ❑ Philosophy with French.

5 Freya failed her exams and **as** ❑ a consequence, had to give up her plans to be a barrister.

6 Because she was so much older, she felt she didn't fit in **to** ❑ the other students.

Exercise 2

Complete the sentences by writing one word in each gap.

lifestyle | self-made | nurture | specialization | ambitious | redundant

1 She is a surgeon – her _____ is hands.

2 When orders started to drop, the company made over 40 people _____.

3 His family isn't wealthy – he is a _____ man.

4 She needs to earn plenty of money to fund her lavish _____.

5 Her drama teacher helped to _____ her talent.

6 My friend, Ruth, has always been highly _____.

Exercise 3

Choose the correct word.

1 I went to Italy in order to immerse **me / myself / I** in the language.

2 Problems at home had a negative impact **in / of / on** Wendi's studies.

3 Peter was made **retired / redundant / sacked** at the age of 50.

4 My new colleagues did their best to make me **feel / seem / make** welcome.

5 Many of these students are **deeply / absolutely / highly** ambitious.

6 Parker soon **showed / found / got** an aptitude for the work.

Exercise 4

Put the correct word in each gap.

| eligible | distinction | aptitude | raised | outsider | excelled |

Scottish lass wins piano prize

Yesterday, Rosie McBride, [1] _____ by her grandparents in the tiny Scottish village of Cairbridge, won the prestigious Chopin Prize for young pianists.

Rosie showed an [2] _____ for music early on. Although her family didn't have much money, they discovered that if she could win a place at a specialist music school, she would be [3] _____ for a grant.

The school Rosie went to was in London. Coming from a small village in Scotland, she says she felt something of an [4] _____, but she loved her studies and [5] _____ at the piano.

Today, Ms McBride is already a pianist of great [6] _____ and is in demand for performances all over the world.

Exercise 5

Put each sentence into the correct order.

1 carpenters who / use the / are self-taught / may not necessarily / best techniques /.

_____

2 a plumber / made redundant / after he was / to retrain as / Michael decided /.

_____

3 nurture the / these specialist camps / talent of / help to / young sportspeople /.

_____

4 of copyright / the area / is in / as a lawyer / her specialization /.

_____

5 service, employees / two days of holiday / after ten years' / an extra / are eligible for /.

_____

6 and will / do anything / my boss is / to get promoted / highly ambitious /.

_____

18

Seeing, hearing, touching, smelling and tasting

Don't touch the cactus – it's very **prickly**!

Look at the table below. It shows which sense these words are connected with. Some words, like **appetizing**, can be used in connection with more than one sense.

Vision	Touch	Smell	Hearing	Taste
appetizing	prickly	appetizing	eavesdrop	appetizing
blurred	slimy	odourless	harmonious	seasoned
harmonious	tickle	stench		
near-/long-sighted	velvety	whiff		
peep				
shadowy				
shimmer				
sparkle				
survey				
visualize				

<table>
<tr><td rowspan="11">Word Finder</td></tr>
</table>

appetizing	ADJECTIVE **Appetizing** food looks and smells good, so that you want to eat it.
blurred	ADJECTIVE A **blurred** shape or image is hard to see clearly because its edges are not distinct.
bystander	NOUN A **bystander** is a person who is present when something happens and who sees it but does not take part in it.
eavesdrop	VERB If you **eavesdrop** on someone, you listen secretly to what they are saying.
harmonious	1 ADJECTIVE Something that is **harmonious** has parts which go well together and which are in proportion to each other. 2 ADJECTIVE Musical notes that are **harmonious** produce a pleasant sound when played together.

Word Finder		
	long-sighted	ADJECTIVE Someone who is **long-sighted** cannot see near things clearly.
	near-sighted / short-sighted	ADJECTIVE Someone who is **near-sighted** or **short-sighted** cannot see distant things clearly.
	odourless	ADJECTIVE An **odourless** substance has no smell.
	peep	VERB If you **peep,** or **peep at** something, you have a quick look at it, often secretly and quietly.
	prickly	ADJECTIVE If something is **prickly**, it has many small, sharp points that you can feel.
	seasoned	ADJECTIVE **Seasoned** food has had salt, pepper, or other spices added to improve its flavour.
	shadowy	ADJECTIVE A **shadowy** figure or shape is someone or something that you can hardly see because they are in a dark place.
	shimmer	VERB If something **shimmers**, it shines with a faint, unsteady light or has an unclear, unsteady appearance.
	slimy	ADJECTIVE **Slimy** substances are thick, wet, and unpleasant. Slimy objects are covered in a **slimy** substance.
	sparkle	1 VERB If something **sparkles**, it is clear and bright and shines with a lot of very small points of light. 2 NOUN **Sparkle** is also a noun.
	stench	NOUN A **stench** is a strong and very unpleasant smell.
	survey	VERB If you **survey** something, you look at or consider the whole of it carefully.
	tickle	VERB When you **tickle** someone, you move your fingers lightly over a sensitive part of their body, often in order to make them laugh.
	velvety	ADJECTIVE Something that is **velvety** feels very soft and smooth.
	visualize	VERB If you **visualize** something, you imagine looking at it in your mind.
	whiff	NOUN If there is a **whiff** of a particular smell, you smell it only slightly or only for a brief period of time, for example, as you walk past someone or something.

Exercise 1

Put each sentence into the correct order.

1 effective and / these cleaning / odourless / materials are / almost completely / .

____

2 from a moving / were taken / the photos / rather blurred / train and are / .

____

3 prickly leaves / by the shrub's / from birds / are protected / the berries / .

____

4 of fish / when we reached / was overwhelming / the quayside / the stench / .

____

5 sparkled in / and the tiny waves / the sunshine / there was / a light breeze / .

____

6 through slimy / opposite river bank / we waded / reach the / mud to / .

____

Exercise 2

Rearrange the letters to find words. Use the definitions to help you.

1 erudoolss _____ (having no smell)

2 rane-tigshde _____ (unable to see things clearly if they are far away)

3 ykripcl _____ (having sharp points)

4 gntzpaiipe _____ (having the appearance of being good to eat)

5 ymisl _____ (having an unpleasant, wet texture)

6 mmhsire _____ (to shine softly)

Exercise 3

Complete the sentences by writing one word in each gap.

seasoned | odourless | harmonious | velvety | appetizing | blurred

1 Patti's tears made everything appear _____.

2 The sounds of the sea, the birdsong and the wind in the trees combined wonderfully into one _____ whole.

3 The glues we use in manufacturing are almost completely _____.

4 The foliage of this shrub has a soft, _____ texture.

5 Sadly, the fatty meat and dry bread we were offered was not particularly _____.

6 The meat was _____ with herbs, fresh from the garden.

Exercise 4

Match the sentence halves.

1 Many innocent bystanders

2 When I feel stressed, I try

3 We strolled through the meadows,

4 Outside our cabin, the lake

5 I caught my brother

6 Max is long-sighted, so

a shimmered in the moonlight.

b to visualize myself in a beautiful forest.

c he needs glasses for reading.

d were injured in the bomb blast.

e eavesdropping at the door.

f the long grasses tickling our legs.

Exercise 5

Choose the correct word or phrase.

1 The warehouse was filled with the stench of **freshly-baked bread / rotting meat / spices**.

2 We could just make out some shadowy **figures / sounds / lights** at the end of the road.

3 We stopped the car to survey the **map / mountain scenery / engine**.

4 Every now and then, we caught a whiff of **fire / music / smoke**.

5 Her **hair / eyes / face** sparkled as she unwrapped her birthday presents.

6 My parents caught me eavesdropping on their **conversation / correspondence / medical records**.

19

Natural phenomena

Read the report about the different natural phenomena:

A major clean-up operation is under way in the capital today, in the **aftermath** of the earth tremors over the weekend that reduced some older buildings to **rubble**. The **death toll** was low, as there were few casualties, but authorities say they have detected continued **seismic activity** in the area, and **aftershocks** continue to be felt across the city.

Due to its proximity to an area of **tectonic plate** movement, the city has excellent emergency measures in place in the event of earthquakes. However, city authorities are now concerned about available water supplies, as the recent **drought** has put increased demands upon reserves, and also the increased risk of **mudslides**. Neighbouring countries have already **pledged support** for a **relief operation** if the alarm is **raised** and one becomes necessary in the event of further tremors. Arrangements have been made for an **air drop** of food and medicine.

Meanwhile to the north of the capital, eruptions are continuing from the steaming crater of the country's biggest volcano, with a steady flow of **molten lava** raising concerns for the safety of small villages close to the volcano.

aftermath	NOUN The **aftermath** of an important event, especially a harmful one, is the situation that results from it.
aftershock	NOUN **Aftershocks** are smaller earthquakes which occur after a large earthquake.
air drop	NOUN An **air drop** is a delivery of supplies by aircraft to an area.
death toll	NOUN The **death toll** of an accident, disaster, or war is the number of people who die in it.
desertification	NOUN **Desertification** is the process by which a piece of land becomes dry, empty, and unsuitable for growing trees or crops on.
drought	NOUN A **drought** is a long period of time during which no rain falls.
grieve	VERB If you **grieve** over something, especially someone's death, you feel very sad about it.
lava flow	NOUN **Lava flow** is the movement of very hot liquid rock coming out of a volcano.
molten lava	NOUN **Molten lava** is very hot liquid rock that comes out of a volcano.

Word Finder

mudslide	NOUN A **mudslide** is a large amount of mud sliding down a mountain, usually causing damage or destruction.
petrified	ADJECTIVE A **petrified** substance or object has gradually turned to stone.
pledge	1 NOUN When someone makes a **pledge**, they make a serious promise that they will do something. 2 VERB When someone **pledges** to do something, they promise in a serious way to do it. When they **pledge** something, they promise to give it.
raise the alarm	PHRASE If you **raise the alarm**, you warn people of danger.
relief operation	NOUN A **relief operation** is an organized attempt to bring help in the form of money, food, or clothing to people in an area that has suffered war or a natural disaster.
rubble	NOUN When a building is destroyed, the pieces of brick, stone, or other materials that remain are referred to as **rubble**.
seismic activity	NOUN **Seismic activity** is the movement of parts of the Earth's crust, for example in an earthquake.
sleet	NOUN **Sleet** is rain that is partly frozen.
stalactite	NOUN A **stalactite** is a long piece of rock which hangs down from the roof of a cave, formed by the slow dripping of water containing minerals.
stalagmite	NOUN A **stalagmite** is a long piece of rock which sticks up from the floor of a cave, formed by the slow dripping of water containing minerals.
tectonic plate	NOUN **Tectonic plates** are the large sections of the Earth's crust.

Word Finder

Exercise 1

Complete the sentences by writing one word or phrase in each gap.

tectonic plates | seismic activity | molten lava | relief operation | death toll | rubble

1 Houses and schools were reduced to _____ in the earthquake.

2 A massive _____ is under way to help survivors of flooding in the region.

3 Astonishingly, it is thought these animals can detect _____ days in advance of an earthquake.

4 An earthquake occurs at a fault line when _____ collide.

5 The _____ has risen to over 420 in the days since the quake.

6 _____ ran downhill from the vents and surface cracks on the eastern side of the volcano.

Exercise 2

For each question, choose the correct answer.

1 What might occur after a major earthquake?
- ❑ aftermaths
- ❑ aftershocks

2 What do you call rain that is partly frozen?
- ❑ sleet
- ❑ rubble

3 What do you call a long piece of hardened minerals which hangs from the ceiling of a cave?
- ❑ stalactite
- ❑ stalagmite

4 When a building is destroyed, what is left behind?
- ❑ rubble
- ❑ lava

5 What do you call a plan to provide assistance, like food, clothing and medicine, to people who have been affected by a natural disaster or war?
- ❑ seismic activity
- ❑ relief operation

Exercise 3

Rearrange the letters to find words. Use the definitions to help you.

1 ificatsedertion _____ (the process by which a piece of land becomes dry, empty and unsuitable for growing plants or crops on)

2 alva wolf _____ (the movement of very hot liquid rock out of a volcano)

3 dieteprif cork _____ (a piece of very old wood that has gradually turned into stone)

4 tietsaltca _____ (a long piece of hardened minerals which hangs from the ceiling of a cave)

5 saltgatime _____ (a long piece of hardened minerals which forms on the floor of a cave)

6 fatrechsok _____ (a smaller earthquake which occurs after a large earthquake)

7 sliddume _____ (a large amount of mud sliding down a mountain, usually causing destruction)

Exercise 4

Match the words and phrases with their definition.

1 death toll	**a**	one of the very large areas of rock forming the earth's crust
2 drought	**b**	a long period of time during which no rain falls
3 molten lava	**c**	the number of people who die in a natural disaster, accident, etc.
4 seismic activity	**d**	movement below the earth's surface, usually the movement of tectonic plates
5 tectonic plate	**e**	the very hot liquid rock that comes out of a volcano

20

The natural world

Good morning ladies and gentlemen and welcome aboard our nature cruise this morning. My name's Steve, and I'm a researcher in **geology**. This area is of particular interest to us geologists because of the **earthquakes** there have been in the region throughout its history, but thankfully there's been no activity for many years!

I'm also an amateur **naturalist**, so I'll be giving you information about the area as we pass through. At the moment, we're getting a great view of the sheer **rocky** sides of the gorge we're passing through. These have been causing concern due to problems with **erosion**, but as you can also see, they provide a fantastic **habitat** for all kinds of water birds. In fact one species that was formerly feared to be **extinct** has recently been found here.

Now, as we leave the gorge behind, we'll come out into an area of arable farming, where you'll see a number of crops being grown, with the emphasis on **sustainable** farming methods. You'll see they make good use of their natural resources here – the **straw** from the fields and **logs** cut from fallen trees are used in house building. Some crops, such as the grape **vines** were almost wiped out by some kind of **bacteria** a few years ago, but now the farms are back to full production. The **spring** water here is said to be particularly good for health, and when the snow begins to **settle** at the beginning of winter, with the breathtaking **mountain range** in the distance, it's an awesome sight.

active	ADJECTIVE An **active** volcano has erupted recently or is expected to erupt quite soon.	
bacteria	NOUN **Bacteria** are very small organisms. Some bacteria can cause disease.	
earthquake	NOUN An **earthquake** is a shaking of the ground caused by movement of the Earth's crust.	
ecology	1 NOUN **Ecology** is the study of the relationships between plants, animals, people, and their environment, and the balances between these relationships.	
	2 NOUN When you talk about the **ecology** of a place, you are referring to the pattern and balance of relationships between plants, animals, people, and the environment in that place.	
ecosystem	NOUN An **ecosystem** is all the plants and animals that live in a particular area together with the complex relationship that exists between them and their environment.	
erosion	NOUN **Erosion** is the gradual destruction and removal of rock or soil in a particular area by rivers, the sea, or the weather.	
extinct	ADJECTIVE A species of animal or plant that is **extinct** no longer has any living members, either in the world or in a particular place.	
extinction	NOUN The **extinction** of a species of animal or plant is the death of all its remaining living members.	
geology	1 NOUN **Geology** is the study of the Earth's structure, surface, and origins.	
	2 NOUN The **geology** of an area is the structure of its land, together with the types of rocks and minerals that exist within it.	
habitat	NOUN The **habitat** of an animal or plant is the natural environment in which it normally lives or grows.	
iceberg	NOUN An **iceberg** is a large tall mass of ice floating in the sea.	
log	NOUN A **log** is a piece of a thick branch or of the trunk of a tree that has been cut so that it can be used for fuel or for making things.	
naturalist	NOUN A **naturalist** is a person who studies plants, animals, insects, and other living things.	
palm	NOUN A **palm** or a **palm tree** is a tree that grows in hot countries. It has long leaves growing at the top, and no branches.	
range	NOUN A **range** of mountains or hills is a line of them.	
rocky	ADJECTIVE A **rocky** place is covered with rocks or consists of large areas of rock and has nothing growing on it.	
settle	VERB If something **settles**, it sinks slowly down and becomes still.	
spring	NOUN A **spring** is a place where water comes up through the ground. **Spring water** is the water that comes from a spring.	
straw	NOUN **Straw** consists of the dried, yellowish stalks from crops such as wheat or barley.	
sustainable	ADJECTIVE You use **sustainable** to describe the use of natural resources when this use is kept at a steady level that is not likely to damage the environment.	
vine	NOUN A **vine** is a plant that grows up or over things, especially one which produces grapes.	

Word Finder

Exercise 1

Put the correct word in each gap.

naturalists | extinct | habitat | Geology | erosion | extinction

One of Britain's leading [1] _____, Steve Sewell, is particularly concerned about the region. Sewell, who knows a thing or two about cliffs, being Professor of [2] _____ at Oxford, says coastal [3] _____ is happening at an alarmingly fast rate. And as the cliffs crumble into the sea, the natural [4] _____ for many seabirds is disappearing too. 'It's likely that in 20 years' time, up to 50 per cent of Britain's seabirds will be facing [5] _____,' says Sewell. 'Even familiar birds, such as the giant egret, may well be [6] _____.'

Exercise 2

Match the sentence halves.

1 She does research into sustainable

2 The snow was now

3 Southern Norway is known for its rocky

4 What had been a small area of forest was now

5 Mauna Loa is one of earth's most active

6 There are thousands of kinds of

a volcanoes, having erupted 33 times since 1843.

b bacteria, most of which are harmless to humans.

c settling, forming a thick white blanket on the ground.

d forms of agriculture.

e a huge pile of neatly stacked logs.

f coastline.

Exercise 3

Complete the sentences by writing one word in each gap.

palms | ecosystem | icebergs | ranges | earthquake | vines

1 The room started to shake, books tumbled off the bookcase, and I realized, to my horror, that it was an _____.

2 Human activity can upset the delicate _____ of a river or lake and harm plant life.

3 Melting _____ are causing sea levels to rise across the globe.

4 The Himalayas is one of the most famous mountain _____ in the world.

5 The _____ along the beach swayed gently in the sea breeze.

6 The grapes were ripening on the _____.

Exercise 4

Match the two parts.

1	an animal's natural	**a**	habitat
2	an active	**b**	volcano
3	melting	**c**	energy
4	mountain	**d**	icebergs
5	sustainable forms of	**e**	ranges

Exercise 5

Rearrange the letters to find words. Use the definitions to help you.

1 riacabet _____ (very small organisms, some of which can cause disease)

2 loogcey _____ (the study of the relationships between plants, animals, people and their environment, and the balance between these relationships)

3 prgins _____ (a place where water comes up through the ground)

4 tarws _____ (the dried, yellowish stalks from crops such as wheat or barley)

5 yeoggol _____ (the study of the earth's structure, surface and origins)

6 metsoceys _____ (all the plants and animals that live in a particular area, together with the complex relationship that exists between them and their environment)

Exercise 6

For each question, tick the correct answer.

1 Which of these means the study of the earth's structure?
- ❑ geology
- ❑ ecosystem
- ❑ ecology

2 Which of these means the gradual removal of rock or soil in a particular area?
- ❑ ecology
- ❑ erosion
- ❑ extinction

3 Which of these words often comes after 'mountain'?
- ❑ range
- ❑ palm
- ❑ log

4 Which of these adjectives can be used to refer to a volcano?
- ❑ sustainable
- ❑ active
- ❑ rocky

5 What do grapes grow on?
- ❑ a palm
- ❑ a log
- ❑ a vine

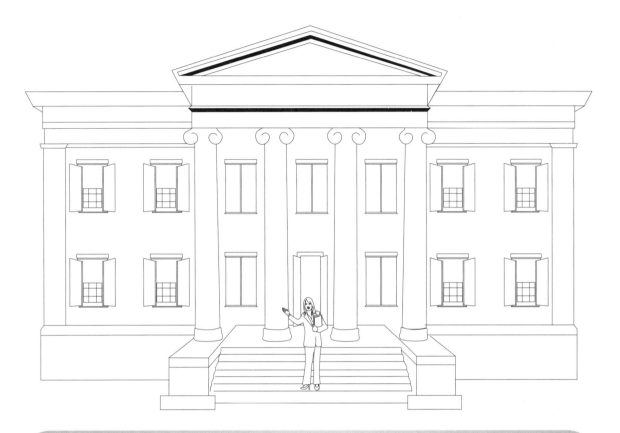

House and home

Now in direct contrast to the **semi-detached** houses we've seen so far, this **mansion** is in a **prime location**. If we just go in through this lovely **porch** and open the front door, you'll see in front of you a magnificent oak **staircase** sweeping up to the landing. The house has a **fitted kitchen** with **built-in cupboards** and all **appliances**, and **fitted carpets** throughout. The gorgeous **open fireplace** downstairs in the **lounge** is one of the many **period features** that were retained during its **reconstruction** in the early 1900s – and that goes for the wonderful oak **beams**, too. And there's plenty of **attic** space, if you wanted to put in a **loft conversion**. Quite an upmarket **dwelling**, I think you'll agree – the perfect place to **settle down** with a family.

Word Finder

appliance	NOUN An **appliance** is a device or machine in your home that you use to do a job such as cleaning or cooking. Appliances are often electrical.
attic (loft)	NOUN An **attic** is a room at the top of a house just below the roof.
beam	NOUN A **beam** is a long thick bar of wood, metal, or concrete, especially one used to support the roof of a building.
built-in cupboard	NOUN A **built-in cupboard** is built as part of a room, rather than being a separate piece of furniture that can be moved.
complex	NOUN A **complex** is a group of buildings designed for a particular purpose, or one large building divided into several smaller areas.

dwelling	NOUN A **dwelling** is a place where someone lives.
fitted carpet	NOUN A **fitted carpet** is cut to the same shape as a room so that it covers the floor completely.
fitted kitchen	NOUN A **fitted kitchen** is designed to fill a particular space and has all its parts fixed in place.
landing	NOUN In a house or other building, the **landing** is the area at the top of the staircase which has rooms leading off it.
loft conversion	NOUN A **loft conversion** is a room in a house, such as an additional bathroom or bedroom, that has been converted from the empty loft space just below the roof.
lounge	NOUN In a house, a **lounge** is a room where people sit and relax.
mansion	NOUN A **mansion** is a very large house.
open fireplace	NOUN An **open fireplace** is a space inside a room where a wood or coal fire can burn.
penthouse	NOUN A **penthouse** or a **penthouse** apartment or suite is a luxurious flat or set of rooms at the top of a tall building.
period feature	NOUN **Period features** are things in a house, such as fireplaces or wall or ceiling decorations, that are typical of an earlier time in history, especially the time when the house was first built.
porch	NOUN A **porch** is a sheltered area at the entrance to a building. It has a roof and sometimes has walls.
prime location	NOUN A **prime location** is one where many people want to live because it has many advantages.
reconstruction	NOUN The **reconstruction** of a building, structure, or road is the activity of building it again, because it has been damaged.
semi-detached	ADJECTIVE A **semi-detached** house is a house that is joined to another house on one side by a shared wall.
settle down	PHRASAL VERB If you **settle down**, you start living in a place where you intend to live for a long time.
staircase	NOUN A **staircase** is a set of stairs inside a building.

Exercise 1

Complete the sentences by writing one word or phrase in each gap.

| built-in | reconstruction | period features | staircase | semi-detached | lounge |

1 Work has begun on the _____ of homes damaged in the fire.

2 We were just chilling in the _____, watching a DVD.

3 We live in a _____ house and, unfortunately, our neighbours are really noisy.

4 He tripped as he was walking down the old wooden _____.

5 There are no _____ cupboards anywhere, so we have nowhere to store our stuff.

6 This house boasts a number of _____, including two open fireplaces and exposed beams in the master bedroom.

Exercise 2

Match the sentence halves.

1 I don't suppose he'll ever settle down

2 She met some playboy who lives in a huge mansion

3 Some 3,500 new dwellings

4 We got a carpenter to make some built-in cupboards

5 She lives in a fabulous Manhattan penthouse

6 You could always convert the loft

a are planned for the region.

b out in the country, with a swimming pool and tennis courts.

c at the top of a twenty-storey tower.

d and get married and have kids.

e into a third bedroom.

f for storage.

Exercise 3

Put the correct word or phrase in each gap.

| appliances | fitted carpets | open fireplace | prime location | beams | period features |

The house we're renting at the moment is a real mixture of the old and the new. There are a few [1]_____ from the eighteenth century – for example, a beautiful [2]_____ in the sitting room (*very* cosy in the winter – it gives off a lot of heat!). You can see the original wooden [3]_____ on some of the ceilings too. The place has lots of character. The kitchen, on the other hand, is full of modern [4]_____ – a dishwasher, microwave and so on. And although there are old wooden floorboards downstairs, the bedrooms all have [5]_____. We're in a [6]_____ too, as the estate agents would say – just by the river in the posh part of town.

Exercise 4

Rearrange the letters to find words. Use the definitions to help you.

1 naimsno _____ (a very large house)

2 plaapince _____ (a device or machine in your home that you use to do a job such as cleaning or cooking)

3 doirep tureafes _____ (parts of an old house that date from the time when the house was originally built)

4 tarsisace _____ (a set of steps inside a building)

5 uelong _____ (a room where people sit and relax)

6 tetfid _____ (describes a piece of furniture, for example a cupboard, that is designed to fill a particular space and is fixed in place)

22

Places and buildings

I really love the town where I live. It's ancient, beautiful, and full of a variety of buildings and places, all very different from each other. If you look up on the hills above the town, you'll see the old **monastery** where monks still live. There's quite a **panorama** to be seen from up there, out to sea. The building's **façade** is stunning – old columns and statues – but there is now **double glazing** throughout the building. There's an **orphanage** up there, too. They're both mentioned in some old **archives**, dating back centuries.

The town itself has changed quite a lot, I guess, since the monastery was built. Now a lot of the old **inns** have become **gastro-pubs**, and there's a **brewery** in town, too – a bit of an **eyesore**, actually, and it smells quite bad some days! There's a great new **aquarium** to visit, and the old **docks** have been cleaned up. There's a very attractive **quay** there now, where small boats moor. There's also an army **barracks** close to here, so the town's often full of soldiers, which gives the place a really lively feel.

My family run a **dairy** just outside of town. We overlook a huge **reservoir** where all our fresh water comes from, so it's a perfect rural **setting** really – but then I come into the old town when I need a change!

Word Finder		
	aquarium	NOUN An **aquarium** is a building, often in a zoo, where fish and underwater animals are kept.
	archives	NOUN **Archives** are a collection of documents and records that contain historical information.
	atrium	NOUN An **atrium** is a part of a building such as a hotel or shopping centre, which extends up through several floors of the building and often has a glass roof.
	barracks	NOUN A **barracks** is a building or group of buildings where members of the armed forces live.
	brewery	NOUN A **brewery** is a place where beer is made.
	cul-de-sac	NOUN A **cul-de-sac** is a short road which is closed off at one end.
	dairy	NOUN A **dairy** is a farm or business that produces milk and products made from milk, such as cream and butter.
	depot	NOUN A **depot** is a place where large amounts of raw materials, equipment, arms, or other supplies are kept until they are needed.
	dock	NOUN A **dock** or **docks** is an enclosed area in a harbour where ships are loaded, unloaded, and repaired.
	double glazing	NOUN If someone has **double glazing** in their house, their windows are fitted with two layers of glass. People put in **double glazing** in order to keep buildings warmer or to keep out noise.
	eyesore	NOUN You describe a building or place as an **eyesore** when it is extremely ugly and you dislike it or disapprove of it.

façade	NOUN The **façade** of a building, especially a large one, is its front wall or the wall that faces the street.
gastro-pub	NOUN A **gastro-pub** is a pub that serves high quality food as well as drinks.
inn	NOUN An **inn** is a small hotel or pub, usually an old one.
monastery	NOUN A **monastery** is a building or collection of buildings in which monks live.
orphanage	NOUN An **orphanage** is a place where orphans live and are looked after.
panorama	NOUN A **panorama** is a view in which you can see a long way over a wide area of land, usually because you are on high ground.
quay	NOUN A **quay** is a long platform beside the sea or a river where boats can be tied up and loaded or unloaded.
reservoir	NOUN A **reservoir** is a lake that is used for storing water before it is supplied to people.
setting	NOUN A particular **setting** is a particular place or type of surroundings where something is or takes place.

Word Finder

Exercise 1

Rearrange the letters to find words or phrases. Use the definitions to help you.

1 leodub gizalng _____ (two layers of glass that are fitted to a window in order to keep a building warm or keep out noise)

2 mitaru _____ (a part of a building such as a hotel or shopping centre, which extends up through several floors of the building and often has a glass roof)

3 irvoseerr _____ (a man-made lake that is used for storing water before it is supplied to people)

4 yaqu _____ (a long platform beside the sea or a river where boats can be tied up and loaded or unloaded)

5 tedop _____ (a place where large amounts of raw materials, equipment, arms or other supplies are kept until they are needed)

6 rewyber _____ (a place where beer is made)

Exercise 2

Choose the correct word.

1 Her parents died when she was a baby and she was raised in **an orphanage / a monastery**.

2 This is the least attractive part of town. The whole area is an utter **façade / eyesore**.

3 Children can visit this working **dairy / brewery** and see cheese and cream being made.

4 Military personnel are accommodated at the nearby **barracks / archives**.

5 The rebels say they have seized control of a government arms **depot / reservoir** in the desert.

6 Since the water is controlled from the nearby **reservoir / aquarium**, there is always a supply.

Exercise 3

For each question, tick the correct answer.

1 An aquarium is
- ☐ a building, often in a zoo, where fish and underwater animals are kept.
- ☐ a room, usually in a gym, where there is a swimming pool.

2 A cul-de-sac is
- ☐ a short road which is closed off at one end.
- ☐ an area of land which goes down suddenly to a lower level.

3 A panorama is
- ☐ a large area of flat grassy land where there are no trees, especially in Eastern Europe.
- ☐ a view in which you can see a long way over a wide area of land, usually from a high place.

4 An orphanage is
- ☐ a place where children with no parents live and are looked after.
- ☐ a large underground channel that carries waste matter and rain water away.

5 A monastery is
- ☐ a quiet, isolated place that you go to in order to rest or improve your health.
- ☐ a building or collection of buildings in which monks live.

6 An inn is
- ☐ a small hotel or pub, usually an old one.
- ☐ a sudden, sharp bend in a road or path.

Exercise 4

Put the correct word in each gap.

| monastery | panorama | quay | setting | gastro-pubs | brewery |

Hillside is a charming eighteenth-century country cottage, offering a stunning

1_____ of the coast. Set within three acres of land, and overlooking the

Victorian seaside town of Burton, Hillside's location is a delight in all seasons. It is the perfect

2_____ for a weekend getaway or a relaxing break. There is plenty to see and

explore in the surrounding area, too. Visit the ancient 3_____ of St Catherine's,

where the monks still live and practise their religion. (St Catherine's boasts a working

4_____ where the monks produce beer based on a recipe dating back to the

fifteenth century.) If food is more your thing, Burton has two of the best 5_____

in the region, and if a leisurely stroll by the sea is what you're after, take a walk along the

6_____ and watch the fishing boats come in with their daily catch.

23

Prefixes and suffixes

There are a number of words in English that have *affixes* – either *prefixes*, before the core word, or *suffixes*, after the core word. Some of the words have both.

Look at the table below. It gives an indication of the meaning of some prefixes that occur before core words.

Prefix	Meaning	Example
bi	two	bilingual
counter	against	counteract
de	take away	deodorant
dis	negative	disadvantage
hyper	excessive	hyperactive
in	negative	inedible
infra	below, beneath	infrastructure
inter	between	interactive
mono	one	monolingual
multi	many	multilateral
non-	not	non-existent
out	better, more	outnumber
over	too much	overwhelming

My younger brother Yannis is amazing! He's as **changeable** as the weather – running around one minute, tired out the next. His room is full of stuff – **countless** computer games and a **never-ending** supply of biscuits and fruit in his top drawer. Mum gives him those, I think. Everyone at school likes him – they all look forward to his **humorous** stories and jokes, even his teacher. But she knows he's very **conscientious** too, so she's not too strict with him!

Word Finder

bilingual	1 ADJECTIVE **Bilingual** means involving or using two languages.	
	2 ADJECTIVE Someone who is **bilingual** can speak two languages equally well, usually because they learned both languages as a child.	
changeable	ADJECTIVE Someone or something that is **changeable** is likely to change many times.	
conscientious	ADJECTIVE Someone who is **conscientious** is very careful to do their work properly.	
counteract	VERB To **counteract** something means to reduce its effect by doing something that produces an opposite effect.	
countless	ADJECTIVE **Countless** means very many.	
deodorant	NOUN **Deodorant** is a substance that you can use on your body to hide or prevent the smell of sweat.	

disadvantaged	ADJECTIVE People who are **disadvantaged** or live in **disadvantaged** areas live in bad conditions and tend not to get a good education or have a reasonable standard of living.
exhaustive	ADJECTIVE If you describe a study, search, or list as **exhaustive**, you mean that it is very thorough and complete.
humorous	ADJECTIVE If someone or something is **humorous**, they are amusing, especially in a clever or witty way.
hyperactive	ADJECTIVE Someone who is **hyperactive** is unable to relax and is always moving about or doing things.
inedible	ADJECTIVE If you say that something is **inedible**, you mean you cannot eat it, for example because it tastes bad or is poisonous.
infrastructure	NOUN The **infrastructure** of a country, society, or organization consists of the basic facilities such as transport, communications, power supplies, and buildings, which enable it to function.
interactive	1 ADJECTIVE An **interactive** computer program or television system is one which allows direct communication between the user and the machine. 2 ADJECTIVE If you describe a group of people or their activities as **interactive**, you mean that the people communicate with each other.
invaluable	ADJECTIVE If you describe something as **invaluable**, you mean that it is extremely useful.
monolingual	ADJECTIVE **Monolingual** means involving, using, or speaking one language.
multilateral	ADJECTIVE **Multilateral** means involving at least three different groups of people or nations.
never-ending	ADJECTIVE If you describe something bad or unpleasant as **never-ending**, you are emphasizing that it seems to last a very long time.
non-existent	ADJECTIVE If you say that something is **non-existent**, you mean that it does not exist when you feel that it should.
outnumber	VERB If one group of people or things **outnumbers** another, the first group has more people or things in it than the second group.
overwhelming	ADJECTIVE If something is **overwhelming**, it affects you very strongly, and you do not know how to deal with it.

Word Finder

Work on your Vocabulary Advanced (C1)

Exercise 1

For each question, tick the correct answer.

1 Someone who speaks two languages fluently is
   ❏ bilingual.
   ❏ monolingual.
   ❏ multilateral.

2 I can't cope with my friend's children – they're
   ❏ never-ending.
   ❏ hyperactive.
   ❏ exhaustive.

3 Vera's proven herself to be ... to the team. They couldn't do without her now.
   ❏ conscientious
   ❏ overwhelming
   ❏ invaluable

4 Ivan has had ... quarrels with the police.
   ❏ disadvantaged
   ❏ countless
   ❏ humorous

5 The food at this place is pretty ... . It depends on the chef.
   ❏ inedible
   ❏ non-existent
   ❏ changeable

Exercise 2

Put the correct word in each gap.

| changeable | infrastructure | counteract | interactive | outnumber |
| countless | bilingual |

The town of East Culton is situated on the north-west coast of the mainland. It has a strong
[1]_____ and is well-serviced by road and rail links. With a population of 50,000,
females [2]_____ males by a ratio of two to one. Most people in the area are
[3]_____ English and Welsh speakers. The town has several points of interest for the
visitor, including an [4]_____ science museum and a large park. Social problems
include a higher than average level of unemployment and in order to [5]_____
this issue, the local government is offering incentives to local industries willing to take on
apprentices. The climate in this part of the country is [6]_____, with frequent rain and
cool summers.

Exercise 3

Rearrange the letters to find words. Use the definitions to help you.

1 vlbniuaale _____ (extremely useful)

2 viphyraecte _____ (constantly active, possibly disruptive)

3 husxavteie _____ (complete, including everything)

4 lllaeiumttra _____ (agreed upon or contributed to by three or more parties)

5 ddeoaontr _____ (something you put on the body to avoid smelling unpleasant)

6 gmnihewlvore _____ (something that has a strong effect or a large number)

Exercise 4

Are the highlighted words correct or incorrect in the sentences?

1 Anand's written a really **humorous** ❑ piece for the students' newspaper. He needs to stop taking himself so seriously.

2 Ir's easier to teach a **monolingual** ❑ group of students, because they make similar errors which you can work on in class.

3 Inner-city children are often **disadvantaged** ❑ when it comes to access to sporting facilities. There aren't enough to go round.

4 Big waves are **non-existent** ❑ at this time of year – great if you're into surfing!

5 The city has rather a weak **infrastructure** ❑. There are few reliable services for residents.

6 Lauren is extremely **conscientious** ❑. She never gets her work in on time.

Exercise 5

Decide if the pairs of sentences have the same meaning.

1 A I've asked you countless times to tidy your room! ❑
  B I don't know how many times I have asked you to tidy your room.

2 A This food is completely inedible. ❑
  B It is quite possible to eat this food.

3 A She told me this never-ending tale about something that happened on holiday. I nearly fell asleep! ❑
  B I was bored by the very long story she told me about her holiday.

4 A The weather's very changeable. You never know what to put on. ❑
  B I find it difficult to know what to wear, because the weather's so unpredictable.

5 A I'm quite into these new interactive teaching methods. The students get so much more out of their lessons. ❑
  B My lessons are going so much better now that the students have become used to the new interactive methods of teaching.

24

Social and political issues

My name's Sofia and I'm studying social and political history at university. So I spend quite a lot of my time in the library, reading about things like the US **Constitution**, the **Declaration** of Independence, and the European **Convention** on Human Rights. It's fascinating. I've got several projects to work on at the moment, like how women won **the vote**, divisions between **working class** and **upper class** people, and a detailed study of the make-up of the British parliament – who is in **power** and who's in **the opposition**, who its **elder statesmen** are, the leaders' **deputies**, any current **diplomatic** rows, and also the history of **socialists** in Europe.

My brother did a history degree and he's given me a book on the **causes** of **anti-social** behaviour, like being **homeless**. It seems that's never gone away. Anyway, the other students on the course are cool – I've got quite a lot **in common with** lots of them whether they're **left wing** or **right wing** politically. And I must admit, I do succumb to **peer pressure** when it's time to go out and have a good time. But I deserve it after all my hard work!

anti-social	ADJECTIVE **Anti-social** behaviour is annoying or upsetting to other people.	
cause	1 NOUN The **cause** of an event, usually a bad event, is the thing that makes it happen. 2 NOUN A **cause** is an aim or principle which a group of people supports or is fighting for.	
constitution	NOUN The **constitution** of a country or organization is the system of laws which formally states people's rights and duties.	
convention	NOUN A **convention** is an official agreement between countries or groups of people.	
declaration	NOUN A **declaration** is an official announcement or statement.	
defence	NOUN **Defence** is the organization of a country's armies and weapons, and their use to protect the country or its interests.	
deputy	NOUN A **deputy** is the second most important person in an organization such as a business or government department. Someone's deputy often acts on their behalf when they are not there.	
diplomatic	ADJECTIVE **Diplomatic** means relating to diplomacy and diplomats.	
elder statesman	NOUN An **elder statesman** is an old and respected politician or former politician who still has influence because of his or her experience.	
have something in common	PHRASE If you **have** something **in common** with someone, you share the same interests or experiences.	
homeless	ADJECTIVE **Homeless** people have nowhere to live.	

Word Finder

left / right wing	ADJECTIVE You can refer to people who support the political ideals of socialism as **left wing.** They are often contrasted with **right wing** people, who support the political ideals of capitalism and conservatism.
liberal	1 ADJECTIVE Someone who has **liberal** views believes people should have a lot of freedom in deciding how to behave and think.
	2 ADJECTIVE A **liberal** system allows people or organizations a lot of political or economic freedom.
middle class	ADJECTIVE **Middle class** people are people who do intellectual or office work such as managers, doctors, lawyers, and teachers.
opposition	NOUN **The opposition** is the political parties or groups that are opposed to a government.
peer pressure	NOUN If someone does something because of **peer pressure**, they do it because other people in their social group do it.
power	NOUN If people **take power** or **come to power**, they take charge of a country's affairs. If a group of people are **in power**, they are in charge of a country's affairs.
socialist	NOUN A **socialist** is a person who believes in a set of political principles whose general aim is to give everyone an equal opportunity to benefit from a country's wealth, for example by having a country's main industries owned by the state.
status	1 NOUN Your **status** is your social or professional position.
	2 NOUN **Status** is the importance and respect that someone has among the public or a particular group.
status symbol	NOUN A **status symbol** is something that a person has or owns that shows they have money or importance in society.
upper class	ADJECTIVE **Upper class** people are the richest people in society who own a lot of property and may not need to work.
vote	NOUN If you have **the vote**, you have the right to vote in an election.
working class	ADJECTIVE **Working class** people are people who do physical work and who do not own much property.

Word Finder

Exercise 1

Complete the sentences by writing one word or phrase in each gap.

1 Anna's quite _____ in her views. She's very open to new ideas.

2 Klaus reluctantly gave in to _____ and did what his mates told him to do.

3 Paolo's new car's a bit of a _____. He must be having a mid-life crisis.

4 Please stop making all that noise in the street! It's extremely _____ behaviour.

5 Sheila and I have very little _____ with each other. I don't know why we're friends!

6 Do you think the Government should cut spending on _____ in peacetime?

Exercise 2

Put the correct word or phrase in each gap.

status | constitution | socialist | elder statesman | liberal | diplomatic | declaration

1 The laws and principles a government must follow: _____

2 An offical announcement, often written: _____

3 Relating to relations between countries: _____

4 An experienced and respected politician: _____

5 Open to new ideas and ready to abandon traditional ways: _____

6 Believing in a system that shares things equally between people: _____

Exercise 3

Match the sentence halves.

1 The Opposition consists of   **a** in support of parties on the right of the political spectrum.

2 Peer pressure is   **b** the usual way of doing something.

3 Anti-social means   **c** a social position within a group.

4 Status means   **d** one or more political parties that are against the government.

5 Convention is   **e** behaving in a way that upsets others.

6 Right wing means   **f** when people in a similar situation to you influence your ideas.

Exercise 4

For each question, tick the correct answer.

1 If you have nowhere to live, you are
   ❑ anti-social.
   ❑ homeless.
   ❑ working class.

2 If you have nothing in common with someone, you
   ❑ don't get on well with them.
   ❑ don't spend time together.
   ❑ don't share the same opinions and interests.

3 An aim or principle which a group of people supports or is fighting for is
   ❑ a cause.
   ❑ a vote.
   ❑ a deputy.

4 Democracy means people are given
   ❑ status symbols.
   ❑ conventions.
   ❑ the vote.

5 A person who is second in command is
   ❑ an elder statesman.
   ❑ a deputy.
   ❑ middle class.

25

Words and phrases for linking ideas

Tom and Marta are both law students and are talking about a seminar they need to prepare for.

Marta	So, Tom – ready to discuss the case study for tomorrow's law seminar?
Tom	Well, I've worked through it, and **by and large** I understand it but it's heavy going, and **on top of that**, I'm not that familiar with the jargon.
Marta	**All the same**, we have to prepare it for tomorrow. **Otherwise** the seminar will be a nightmare, **in a word**.
Tom	OK, well, let's see ... the lawyer's client – let's call him Mr X – was owed some money by one of his customers, Mrs Y, and took action **accordingly**. He consulted his lawyer about legal proceedings. **Nonetheless** the lawyer counselled caution. Yes, the woman owed him a sizeable sum for some books he'd sold her on the internet, but **for all that**, the lawyer warned against going to court.
Marta	Hmm, he feared negative repercussions, **namely** damage to Mr X's reputation. **Better**, he felt, to explore other avenues first. **Moreover**, he was concerned that Mrs Y might have a case against Mr X – she had **correspondingly** alleged that the books she'd bought from him were of very poor quality – not fit for purpose, **in short**.
Tom	Hmm ... **mind you**, if the enclosed photos were accurate, she had a point. They were quite worn, **whereas** he'd apparently told her they were brand new.
Marta	... Or **rather**, 'in very good condition', as he'd written in the seller's description...

<table>
<tr><td rowspan="9" style="vertical-align:middle">Word Finder</td></tr>
<tr><td>accordingly</td><td>ADVERB If you consider a situation and then act accordingly, the way you act depends on the nature of the situation.</td></tr>
<tr><td>all the same</td><td>PHRASE You can say all the same to introduce a statement which indicates that a situation has not changed, in spite of what has just been said.</td></tr>
<tr><td>better</td><td>ADJECTIVE You can say that it is better to do something when you are advising someone to do it.</td></tr>
<tr><td>by and large</td><td>PHRASE If something is true by and large, it is generally true.</td></tr>
<tr><td>conversely</td><td>ADVERB You say conversely to indicate that the situation you are about to describe is the opposite or reverse of the one you have just described.</td></tr>
<tr><td>correspondingly</td><td>ADVERB You use correspondingly when describing a situation which is closely connected with one you have just mentioned or is similar to it.</td></tr>
<tr><td>for all that</td><td>PHRASE You can use for all that when you accept that something is true, but want to introduce another statement which partly contradicts it.</td></tr>
</table>

in a word	PHRASE You can use **in a word** when you are going to describe a situation in one word or in a very short phrase.
in the same way	PHRASE You use **in the same way** when mentioning a fact or situation that is similar to the one that you have just mentioned.
likewise	ADVERB You use **likewise** when you are comparing two methods, states, or situations and saying that they are similar.
mind you	PHRASE You use **mind you** to emphasize a piece of information that you are adding, especially when this explains what you have said or contradicts it.
moreover	ADVERB You use **moreover** to introduce a piece of information that adds to or supports the previous statement.
namely	ADVERB You use **namely** to introduce detailed information about the subject you are discussing, or a particular aspect of it.
nonetheless	ADVERB You use **nonetheless** when saying something that contrasts with what has just been said.
on top of that	PHRASE You can use **on top of that** to indicate that a particular problem exists in addition to a number of other problems.
otherwise	ADVERB You use **otherwise** after stating a situation or fact, in order to say what the result or consequence would be if this situation or fact was not the case.
rather	ADVERB You use **rather** when you are correcting something that you have just said, especially when you are describing a particular situation after saying what it is not.
thus	ADVERB You use **thus** to show that what you are about to mention is the result or consequence of something else that you have just mentioned.
whereas	CONJUNCTION You use **whereas** to introduce a comment which contrasts with what is said in the main clause.

(Word Finder)

Exercise 1

Choose the correct word or phrase.

Course outline: 20th century literature

The purpose of this short course is not to cover every aspect of 20th century literature.
[1]**Likewise / Rather / Whereas**, it will focus on a few key writers, [2]**namely / thus / conversely** Proust, Kafka, Steinbeck and Woolf.

[3]**Accordingly / Whereas / Otherwise** the two-year course is designed for students who have already studied literature, this course is suitable for beginners, and the level will be set [4]**conversely / namely / accordingly**.

[5]**Whereas / Rather / Nonetheless**, students will be encouraged to produce work of a high standard. [6]**Otherwise / In short / By and large**, this is the perfect introduction to modern literature for the intelligent non-specialist.

Exercise 2

Put the correct word in each gap.

| nonetheless | likewise | otherwise | namely | correspondingly | thus |

Dear Sir,

My wife and I ate at your new restaurant last week. The food was excellent, but our evening was spoiled [1]_____ by several other factors.

Firstly, when paying such high prices, one expects a [2]_____ high level of service. Standards of decoration and cleanliness, [3]_____, should be high. None of these things were the case.

One other issue caused me particular distress, [4]_____ the lack of facilities for the disabled. Huge vases of flowers were positioned at the door to the restaurant, [5]_____ making wheelchair access extremely difficult.

I hope that you will act promptly to make improvements; [6]_____ I fear your new venture will not be successful.

Yours,

Michael Manners

Exercise 3

Which sentences are correct?

1 Jake's brother is very confident, whereas Jake himself is quite shy. ❑

2 Some of our workers are more skilled and thus better paid than others. ❑

3 In real life, nobody is all bad, or, otherwise, all good. ❑

4 Sometimes we were given bread to eat or, better still, pizza. ❑

5 People with more experience were nonetheless given more responsibility. ❑

6 The hall was not intended for concerts, but better for religious worship. ❑

Exercise 4

Match the two parts.

1 Tobias often stays out late.

2 She has her own cook and gardener.

3 Susana did all the driving and cooking on the trip.

4 What did I think of the play?

5 Carol wasn't too much trouble.

6 Being a poet is a lonely life and I have almost no money.

a Mind you, she can afford it.

b For all that, I wouldn't do any other job.

c On top of that, everyone expected her to translate for them too.

d In a word: fantastic!

e By and large, she behaved pretty well.

f All the same, I was worried when he wasn't back by midnight.

26

Crime and law

Types of crime	Detection, arrest and court procedures	Punishments
arson	charge	community service
assault	lie detector	(be) on probation
blackmail	magistrate	a prison sentence
corruption	plead	capital punishment
fraud	(be arrested) on suspicion of	
manslaughter	perjury	
mugging		
white collar crime		
smuggling		
serial killings		

Word Finder

arson	NOUN **Arson** is the crime of deliberately setting fire to a building or vehicle.
assault	NOUN An **assault** on a person is a physical attack on them.
blackmail	NOUN **Blackmail** is the action of threatening to reveal a secret about someone, unless they do something you tell them to do, such as giving you money.
capital punishment	NOUN **Capital punishment** is punishment which involves the legal killing of a person who has committed a serious crime such as murder.
charge	NOUN A **charge** is a formal accusation that someone has committed a crime.
community service	NOUN **Community service** is unpaid work that criminals sometimes do as a punishment instead of being sent to prison.
corruption	NOUN **Corruption** is dishonesty and illegal behaviour by people in positions of authority or power.
fraud	NOUN **Fraud** is the crime of gaining money or financial benefits by a trick or by lying.
lie detector	NOUN A **lie detector** is an electronic machine used mainly by the police to find out whether a suspect is telling the truth.
magistrate	NOUN A **magistrate** is an official who acts as a judge in law courts which deal with minor crimes or disputes.
manslaughter	NOUN **Manslaughter** is the illegal killing of a person by someone who did not intend to kill them.
mugging	NOUN **Mugging** is the crime of attacking someone in the street in order to steal their money or possessions.

on probation	PHRASE If someone is **on probation**, they have committed a crime and have to obey the law and be supervised by a probation officer, rather than being sent to prison.
on suspicion of	PHRASE If someone is arrested **on suspicion of** a particular crime, police think that they may have committed that crime.
perjury	NOUN If someone commits **perjury**, they lie while giving evidence in a court of law.
plead	VERB When someone charged with a crime **pleads** guilty or not guilty in a court of law, they officially state that they are guilty or not guilty of the crime.
prison sentence	NOUN If someone is given a **prison sentence**, they have to spend time in prison for a crime they have committed.
serial	ADJECTIVE **Serial** killings or attacks are a series of killings or attacks committed by the same person. This person is known as a **serial** killer or attacker.
smuggling	NOUN **Smuggling** is the act of taking things or people into a place or out of it illegally or secretly.
white collar crime	NOUN **White collar crime** is committed by people who work in offices, and involves stealing money secretly from companies or the government, for example by creating false records or documents.

Exercise 1

Match the words and phrases with their definition.

1	arson	**a**	obtaining money or making someone do something by threatening to reveal a secret
2	blackmail	**b**	for an offender: being under supervision for a period of time and required not to commit further crimes
3	capital punishment	**c**	an offence committed by someone in connection with their office-based job
4	white collar crime	**d**	intentionally setting fire to something in order to damage it
5	on probation	**e**	the death penalty
6	perjury	**f**	telling a lie in court while under oath

Exercise 2

Rearrange the letters to find words. Use the definitions to help you.

1 rerjpyu _____ (lying in court)

2 slghenaruamt _____ (killing someone by accident)

3 luatsas _____ (violent attack)

4 purnotocir _____ (dishonestly using a position of power)

5 gluegms _____ (move things illegally or secretly)

6 mkiaclalb _____ (get money by threatening to reveal a secret)

Exercise 3

Find the words or phrases that do not belong, as shown.

1 Types of crime

fraud   arson   (magistrate)

2 Verbs connected with crime

plead   assign   commit

3 Criminal actions

collaborating   smuggling   mugging

4 People connected with the law

magistrate   principal   jury

5 Phrases connected with crime

on board   on probation   on suspicion of

6 Categories of crime

white collar   blue collar   red collar

7 Punishments

prison sentence   perjury   community service

8 Violent crimes

corruption   manslaughter   assault

Exercise 4

Choose the correct word.

1 He faces a **crime / charge / defence** of theft.

2 He was a **serial / consecutive / sequential** murderer.

3 The shoplifter was put on **time / condition / probation** for nine months.

4 She **appealed / pleaded / claimed** guilty.

5 There is an increase in **white / black / green** collar crime.

6 Can he refuse to take a lie **detector / control / measurement** test?

Exercise 5

Put the correct word in each gap.

| serial | probation | mugging | sentence | charged | pleads |

Increase in shoplifting

The last year has seen an increase in the number of people being [1]_____ with
shoplifting, even though stores are doing more to try to prevent this type of crime. Interestingly,
other, arguably more serious crimes, such as [2]_____, are decreasing in number.
Store detectives observe the shoplifter and call the police and nine times out of ten the
accused [3]_____ guilty. If it is a first offence, the shoplifter will usually be put on
[4]_____, but if the person is a [5]_____ shoplifter they may receive a
prison [6]_____.

27

Talking about beliefs and ideas

I was brought up in a deeply religious family, so it's rather surprising that I'm an **atheist** now. My wife says I'm too **dogmatic**, and prefers to refer to herself as an **agnostic**, although I think she is a **believer**, really. We're both very **accepting** of each other's beliefs, though, and we also live in an area of great **cultural diversity**, so we've learnt a lot about other beliefs, too. My father has always been a bit **overbearing**, and slightly **obsessive** about religious **ideology**, whereas my mother is fairly **middle-of-the-road**, and keen for us not to become too **fanatical** about anything. She is a very committed **pacifist**, though, and I admire her for that, as she comes from a military family. I think it was a bit of a **culture shock** for her to live outside that environment initially.

accepting	ADJECTIVE	If you are **accepting** of something, you allow it and do not try to change it.
agnostic	NOUN	An **agnostic** believes that it is not possible to know whether God exists or not.
atheist	NOUN	An **atheist** is a person who believes that there is no God.
be all for	PHRASE	If you **are all for** something, you agree with or approve of it.
believer	NOUN	A **believer** is someone who is sure that God exists or that their religion is true.
contrary to popular belief	PHRASE	You can say that **contrary to popular belief** something is not true to mean that it is not true even though many people believe it.
conviction	NOUN	A **conviction** is a strong belief or opinion.
credulous	ADJECTIVE	If you describe someone as **credulous**, you have a low opinion of them because they are too ready to believe what people tell them and are easily deceived.
cultural diversity	NOUN	**Cultural diversity** is a situation in which there are people from many different cultures or backgrounds.
culture shock	NOUN	**Culture shock** is a feeling of anxiety, loneliness, and confusion that people sometimes experience when they first arrive in another country or culture.
dogmatic	ADJECTIVE	If you say that someone is **dogmatic**, you are critical of them because they are convinced that they are right, and refuse to consider that other opinions might also be justified.
ethics	NOUN	**Ethics** are moral beliefs and rules about right and wrong.
fanatical	ADJECTIVE	If you describe someone as **fanatical**, you disapprove of them because you consider their behaviour or opinions to be very extreme.
free will	NOUN	If you believe in **free will**, you believe that people have a choice in what they do and that their actions have not been decided in advance by God or by any other power.
ideology	NOUN	An **ideology** is a set of beliefs, especially the political beliefs on which people, parties, or countries base their actions.

Word Finder

Word Finder	middle-of-the-road	NOUN If someone's opinions are **middle-of-the-road**, they are not at all extreme.
	obsessive	ADJECTIVE If someone's behaviour is **obsessive**, they cannot stop doing a particular thing or behaving in a particular way.
	overbearing	ADJECTIVE An **overbearing** person tries to make other people do what he or she wants in an unpleasant and forceful way.
	pacifist	NOUN A **pacifist** is someone who believes that violence is wrong and refuses to take part in wars.
	premonition	NOUN If you have a **premonition**, you have a feeling that something is going to happen, often something unpleasant.

Exercise 1

Match the words with their definitions.

1 agnostic
2 atheist
3 pacifist
4 dogmatic
5 conviction
6 ethics

a principles of conduct governing an individual or a group
b strongly opposed to conflict and war
c not committed to believing or not believing in God
d expressing opinions strongly, as if they were facts
e believing there is no God
f strong belief

Exercise 2

Put the correct word in each gap.

accepting | belief | diversity | believer | atheist | dogmatic

In this Social Sciences module, we are going to take a typical city high street in the UK and look at the cultural [1]_____ represented there, considering present examples such as the Turkish restaurant and the Chinese supermarket. We are also going to explore different people's attitudes to religion. We will listen to a discussion in which Laura, a strong [2]_____ in Christianity, explains her opinions to Tom, who is an [3]_____ and doesn't believe in God at all. They are very [4]_____ of each other's points of view, but this is not always the case in a community. Difficulties may arise when a person expresses his or her views in a [5]_____ way. Contrary to popular [6]_____, in this community, like so many others, people get on well with each other despite their differences.

Exercise 3

Rearrange the letters to find words. Use the definitions to help you.

1 nomitiernpo _____ (anticipation of an event without conscious reason)
2 nrervgiabeo _____ (tending to overwhelm)
3 sesosebvi _____ (fixated with or overly interested in)
4 scgoaint _____ (unwilling to commit to an opinion about religion)
5 tamocgid _____ (expressing strong beliefs as truths)
6 gleiyood _____ (a set of ideas that a group holds)

Exercise 4

Decide if the pairs of sentences have the same meaning.

1 **A** Mark is strongly in favour of lowering the voting age.
  B Mark is all for lowering the voting age. ☐

2 **A** She holds quite middle-of-the-road views.
  B She holds fanatical views. ☐

3 **A** I'm doing this of my own free will.
  B I'm being forced into doing this. ☐

4 **A** Few people are credulous enough to believe that.
  B Not many people will believe that. ☐

5 **A** They share the conviction that the death penalty is wrong.
  B They both strongly believe that the death penalty is wrong. ☐

Exercise 5

Are the highlighted words correct or incorrect in the sentences?

1 Contrary to **popularist** ☐ belief, most people in this town are not well off.

2 It must be tough, being on the medical **ethics** ☐ committee.

3 When I first moved to Britain, I suffered from culture **distress** ☐, but after a while I got used to British ways.

4 He left of his own free **mind** ☐.

5 She listened **incredulously** ☐ to the poor excuses he made.

6 I had a **premonition** ☐ that we would have an accident.

Exercise 6

Write the correct form of the word in brackets to complete each sentence.

1 He became a _____ (peace) after his experience of war.

2 His _____ (obsess) behaviour became more pronounced as he got older.

3 She doesn't mean to be rude, it's just that she expresses herself rather _____ (dogma).

4 We're firm _____ (believe) in the benefits of adult education.

5 The children suffered, because of their _____ (bear) father.

6 The cutural _____ (diverse) of this neighbourhood makes it a marvellous place to live.

28

News and current affairs

Look at the cutting and the byline, then read the text written by a journalist about his experiences:

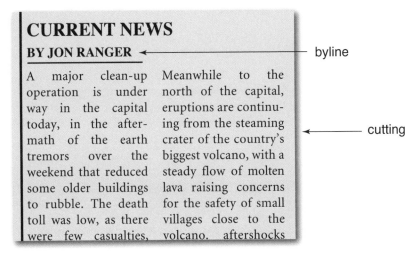

CURRENT NEWS

BY JON RANGER ← byline

A major clean-up operation is under way in the capital today, in the aftermath of the earth tremors over the weekend that reduced some older buildings to rubble. The death toll was low, as there were few casualties, Meanwhile to the north of the capital, eruptions are continuing from the steaming crater of the country's biggest volcano, with a steady flow of molten lava raising concerns for the safety of small villages close to the volcano. aftershocks

← cutting

My name's Jon Ranger – you might have seen my **byline** in various **broadsheet** newspapers. As a trainee reporter I started by writing the **obituaries** – quite interesting, writing about famous people's lives. Then I moved to the news **desk** and started writing **copy** for them. It was really exciting, and I got to the stage where I could fill quite a few **column inches** very quickly!

Of course, you always hope a big story might **break** while you're on duty, and one day it did – and I got my first **scoop**! But then, as the story developed, it got quite controversial, so my editor **killed** it. The **gutter press** had a field day, though. The rival **rag** in my area, a **tabloid newspaper**, picked it up and covered it to death in the end. It was the **silly season**, though, and there wasn't much else going on.

But I hate the move there's been towards **chequebook journalism**, and reducing everything to easily digestible **soundbites**. I think our readers still want some quality in-depth analysis and comment from their paper.

banner	NOUN A **banner** is a large headline or advertisement that stretches across the whole of a newspaper page or website.
break	VERB When a piece of news **breaks**, people hear about it from the newspapers, television, or radio.
broadsheet	NOUN A **broadsheet** is a newspaper that is printed on large sheets of paper. **Broadsheets** are generally considered to be more serious than other newspapers.
byline	NOUN A **byline** is a line at the top of an article in a newspaper or magazine giving the author's name.
caption	NOUN A **caption** is the words printed underneath a picture or cartoon which explain what it is about.
chequebook journalism	NOUN **Chequebook journalism** is the practice of paying people large sums of money for information about crimes or famous people in order to get material for newspaper articles.
column inches	NOUN **Column inches** refers to space in newspapers that is filled by writing about a particular story or subject.
copy	NOUN In journalism, **copy** is written material that is ready to be printed or read in a broadcast.
cutting	NOUN A **cutting** is a piece of writing which has been cut from a newspaper or magazine.
desk	NOUN A particular department of a broadcasting company, or of a newspaper or magazine company, can be referred to as a particular **desk**.
gutter press	NOUN You can refer to newspapers and magazines which print mainly stories about sex and crime as the **gutter press**.
kill a story	PHRASE If a newspaper or someone in charge of it **kills a story**, they do not print it.
masthead	NOUN A newspaper's **masthead** is the part at the top of the front page where its name appears in big letters.
obituary	NOUN Someone's **obituary** is an account of their life and character which is printed in a newspaper or broadcast soon after they die.
paparazzi	NOUN The **paparazzi** are photographers who follow famous people around, hoping to take interesting or shocking photographs that they can sell to a newspaper.
rag	NOUN People refer to a newspaper as a **rag** when they have a poor opinion of it.
scoop	1 NOUN A **scoop** is an exciting news story which is reported in one newspaper or on one television programme before it appears anywhere else. 2 VERB If a newspaper **scoops** other newspapers, it succeeds in printing an exciting or important story before they do.
silly season	NOUN The **silly season** is the time around August when the newspapers are full of unimportant or silly news stories because there is not much political news to report.
soundbite	NOUN A **soundbite** is a short sentence or phrase, usually from a politician's speech, that is repeated a lot in the media because it is easy to understand or remember.
tabloid	NOUN A **tabloid** is a newspaper that has small pages, short articles, and lots of photographs. Tabloids are often considered to be less serious than other newspapers.

Word Finder

Exercise 1

Put the correct word or phrase in each gap.

| silly season | caption | paparazzi | rag | broadsheets | column inches |

It would seem that the love life of the actress Kim Mulder has become a national obsession, judging by the number of tabloid [1]_____ devoted to her recent split from fellow actor Dane Miller. Admittedly, it is summer. We have officially entered the [2]_____ and news is slow, but I counted no less than three pictures of Kim Mulder in one [3]_____ this morning (the [4]_____ are clearly still just as busy in this slow season). The [5]_____ under one rather unflattering shot read, 'Not so slim Kim', which reflects the other tabloid obsession: the actress's recent weight gain. This interest in Mulder isn't confined to the tabloids either. Three [6]_____ feature a picture of her in today's editions.

Exercise 2

For each question, tick the correct answer.

1 A byline is
   - ❏ a line at the top of an article giving the author's name.
   - ❏ a title of a paragraph that is not the main title of the article.

2 A masthead is
   - ❏ a headline that is sensational and designed to attract readers to the paper.
   - ❏ the part at the top of the front page of a newspaper where its name appears in big letters.

3 An obituary is
   - ❏ an account of someone's life and character which is printed in a newspaper soon after they die.
   - ❏ an article in which someone states their opinion of a film, book, exhibition, etc.

4 A scoop is
   - ❏ an exciting news story which is reported in one newspaper before it appears anywhere else.
   - ❏ a journalist who does boring work or work that is of low quality.

5 A soundbite is
   - ❏ a piece of important information which is contained within an article.
   - ❏ a short sentence or phrase, usually from a politician's speech, which is widely reported in the media.

Exercise 3

Match the sentence halves.

1 These days, it seems that news is breaking faster on

2 She works on the news

3 Some recent examples have increased debate about the ethics of

4 The key to becoming a successful journalist is the ability

5 Understandably, he didn't want his private life splashed all over

6 I found some newspaper cuttings

a chequebook journalism.

b social media than it is in actual newsrooms.

c to write good copy.

d the front page of the tabloids.

e on the subject at my local library.

f desk of a national paper.

Exercise 4

Rearrange the letters to find words. Use the definitions to help you.

1 theamads _____ (the part at the top of the front page of a newspaper where its name appears in big letters)

2 batliod _____ (a newspaper that has small pages, short articles and lots of photographs)

3 yleinb _____ (the line at the top of an article in a newspaper or magazine that gives the author's name)

4 cosop _____ (an exciting news story which is reported in one newspaper before it appears anywhere else)

5 lisly aessno _____ (the time around August when newspapers are full of unimportant news stories because there is not much political news to report)

6 tnuictg _____ (a piece of writing which has been cut from a newspaper or magazine)

Exercise 5

Choose the correct word or phrase.

1 The **caption / byline** under the photo read, 'Looters riot in city centre'.

2 The paper claimed it was 'free from party political bias, free from proprietorial influence' in a **banner / masthead** it carried on the front page of its daily edition.

3 In fact, it was the *Mail* that got the **rag / scoop** on the royal engagement, announcing it in their Sunday edition.

4 Eventually, deciding that he couldn't trust his source, the editor decided to **kill / break** the story rather than risk publishing it.

5 The couple divorced in 1999 amid rumours in the **gutter press / paparazzi** about alcoholism and mental ill health.

6 When Wilson's ex-husband got engaged to a 20-something dancer he'd known less than a year, it was all over the **tabloids / broadsheets**.

29

Music and the arts

I'm the **lead violinist** in an orchestra, and I love my job! It's just wonderful to hear everyone playing in **harmony**, and the audience **applauding**, while our conductor keeps us all under control. He **bears a strong resemblance** to my older brother Luke, in many ways – he's quite bossy, too! We're always busy – last week we recorded the **score** for a new film, to accompany the **lyrics** sung by a famous songwriter, and the week before we played in the city art gallery. I was quite distracted by all the beautiful **oil** and **watercolour** paintings that there were there. Some valuable **masterpieces**, certainly. Anyway, that was very successful – no **booing**, and as the last **chords** died away, the whole audience just erupted – stood up and clapped and cheered like mad! Fantastic!

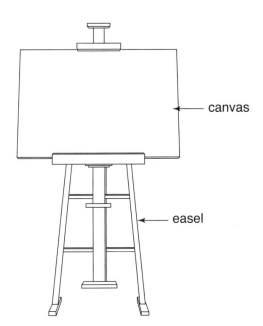

canvas

easel

recording studio

sitter (model)

applaud	VERB When a group of people **applaud**, they clap their hands in order to show approval, for example when they have enjoyed a play or concert.
bear a resemblance	PHRASE If someone or something **bears a resemblance** to someone or something else, they are similar to them.
boo	1 VERB If you **boo** a speaker or performer, you shout 'boo' or make other loud sounds to indicate that you do not like them, their opinions, or their performance. 2 NOUN **Boo** is also a noun.
brush stroke	NOUN A **brush stroke** is a mark made on a surface by the movement of a painter's brush.
canvas	NOUN A **canvas** is a piece of canvas or similar material on which an oil painting can be done.
chord	NOUN A **chord** is a number of musical notes played or sung at the same time with a pleasing effect.
easel	NOUN An **easel** is a wooden frame that supports a picture which an artist is painting or drawing.
harmony	NOUN **Harmony** is the pleasant combination of different notes of music played at the same time.
instrumental	ADJECTIVE **Instrumental** music is performed by instruments and not by voices.
lead violinist	NOUN The **lead violinist** in an orchestra is the most senior violin player, who helps the conductor to lead the orchestra.
lyrics	NOUN The **lyrics** of a song are its words.
masterpiece	NOUN A **masterpiece** is an extremely good painting, novel, film, or other work of art.
oil	1 NOUN **Oils** are thick paints made from coloured powder mixed with oil. 2 NOUN An **oil** or **oil painting** is a painting made using oil paints
orchestra pit	NOUN In a theatre, the **orchestra pit** is the space reserved for the musicians playing the music for an opera, musical, or ballet, immediately in front of or below the stage.
recording artist	NOUN A **recording artist** is a singer or musician who makes recordings.
recording studio	NOUN A **recording studio** is a special room or building where musical recordings are made.
score	NOUN The **score** of a film, play, or similar production is the music which is written or used for it.
sitter	NOUN A **sitter** is someone who poses as a model for an artist.
sketch	NOUN A **sketch** is a drawing that is done quickly without a lot of details. Artists often use **sketches** as a preparation for a more detailed painting or drawing.
still life	NOUN A **still life** is a painting or drawing of an arrangement of objects such as flowers or fruit.
watercolour	1 NOUN **Watercolours** are coloured paints, used for painting pictures, which you apply with a wet brush or dissolve in water first. 2 NOUN A **watercolour** is a picture which has been painted with watercolours.

Word Finder

Exercise 1

For each question, tick the correct answer.

1 Which of these is a wooden frame with legs, which is used to hold a painting?
   - ❏ brush
   - ❏ easel
   - ❏ canvas

2 Which of these is a piece of written music, with parts for all the singers and instrumentalists on separate lines?
   - ❏ score
   - ❏ chord
   - ❏ harmony

3 Which of these is a drawing that is done quickly and without much detail?
   - ❏ sketch
   - ❏ watercolour
   - ❏ sitter

4 Which of these is several musical notes played simultaneously, whether or not the resulting sound is pleasant?
   - ❏ harmony
   - ❏ score
   - ❏ chord

5 Which of these is often an area of a theatre?
   - ❏ lead violinist
   - ❏ recording studio
   - ❏ orchestra pit

Exercise 2

Put the correct word in each gap.

masterpiece	applaud	lead violinist	recording artist	instrumental	lyrics
chords	harmony	boo			

I went to a wonderful concert last week. The soloist was the [1]_____ with an orchestra, who rarely performs solo. However, he's a prolific [2]_____, both with the orchestra and in his own right. Having heard several CDs of his, I was looking forward to hearing him in the flesh, as it were.

The programme was largely [3]_____, although a choir also took part in the final work – a [4]_____ by Mozart, where all the performers played and sang in perfect [5]_____. As the final few [6]_____ faded away, there was a rapt silence for a few seconds, before the audience began to [7]_____ – more enthusiastically than I had ever heard before.

Exercise 3

Which sentences are correct?

1 The portrait that caught my eye was of a man bearing a strong resemblance to my father. ❏

2 The audience was so dumbfounded by the unorthodox production that when the director appeared for a curtain call, he was booed off the stage. ❏

3 I can read music well enough to follow a score – provided it isn't the work of a very avant-garde composer! ❏

4 On the walls were watercolours Jemima had obviously painted herself – still lifes, mainly of fruit and flowers. ❏

5 While the music had a haunting quality that I found beguiling, the lyrics were pedestrian, verging on the banal. ❏

6 John went to look up at the orchestra pit, which was on a platform over the stage. ❏

Exercise 4

Rearrange the letters to find words. Use the definitions to help you.

1 leeas _____ (a wooden frame that supports a picture which an artist is painting or drawing)

2 nmaorhy _____ (a pleasant combination of different notes of music played at the same time)

3 ncvsaa _____ (a piece of material on which an oil painting can be done)

4 tempieesacr _____ (an extremely good painting, book, poem, film, or other work of art)

5 crseo _____ (the written form of a complete piece of music)

6 droch _____ (a number of musical notes played or sung at the same time, often with a pleasing effect)

Exercise 5

Are the highlighted words correct or incorrect in this text?

As the artist showed me into his studio, I was almost overwhelmed by the profusion of objects filling every space in the room – floor, walls, even the windows. An unfinished painting stood on a rickety-looking **easel** ❏, and even to my untutored eye it had the makings of a **masterpiece** ❏. Stacked on the floor were lots of **chords** ❏ – some of them **watercolours** ❏, the majority just pencil **scores** ❏. Of those that were exposed to view, almost all depicted the same **sitter** ❏, an elderly woman shown against a bewildering array of backgrounds.

Metaphorical language

There are a number of words and expressions in which language is used figuratively. This means that words mean something quite different from their normal meaning.

A metaphor says that one thing is another completely unrelated thing, and invites you to make a comparison between the two. Look at the following famous example of a metaphor.

All the world's a stage
And all the men and women merely players
They have their exits and their entrances ...
                    Shakespeare

A Metaphorical Mystery

It happened about a month ago. At the time, I'd been **doggedly** determined to get my life back on track after a break-up with an **old flame** some years before. I hadn't had a job, so she'd been supporting both of us financially, and at the beginning she hadn't seemed to mind working hard and had just **ploughed on** regardless while I studied, mostly my degree subject, but also whatever else **kindled** my interest. But then she'd suddenly seemed to get fed up with what she'd started to see as my **sponging off** her, and that had really **soured** our relationship. Looking back, I guess I hadn't really helped her out much either financially or in any other way, even at a time when she was **swamped** with work. I'd waste the money she'd earned, buying her red roses and such like. I'd found it impossible afterwards to admit the break-up was all my fault, so although when talking with friends I knew they were desperate for me to **spill the beans**, I'd always **draw a veil over** the reasons. As far as they were concerned, the whole thing was **cloaked in mystery**.

Anyway, I was standing at the bus stop one evening trying to catch a bus home. Time was **crawling**. It was pouring with rain, I was soaking wet, absolutely exhausted and feeling somehow **downtrodden**. No buses had come along for ages, so should I call a taxi and spend money I couldn't afford, or walk home and get soaking wet, and possibly sick? I was **between a rock and a hard place**. Just then, a big car pulled up beside me. It was driven by a woman – dark glasses and a scarf covering her head, so I couldn't see her face too clearly. She looked familiar, and yet ... She offered me a lift into town, and I gratefully accepted, putting my bag down beside me in my wet clothes, and giving her a sheepish smile. We didn't talk much during the journey. It was warm inside the car, and I must have fallen asleep, as the time soon **slipped by** and we arrived in the city centre. She stopped the car and I got out, thanking her and taking my bag with me. As she drove off, I looked inside my bag – and suddenly realized my wallet was missing. In its place was one single red rose. Hmm – had I **been taken for a ride**?

between a rock and a hard place	PHRASE If you are **between a rock and a hard place**, you are in a difficult situation because you have to choose one of two equally bad things.
cloaked in mystery	PHRASE If something is **cloaked in mystery**, people cannot understand it or know about it because it is secret or not explained.
crawl	VERB If you say that time **crawls**, you mean that it seems to pass extremely slowly.
downtrodden	ADJECTIVE People who are **downtrodden** are treated very badly by people with power, and do not have the ability or the energy to do anything about it.
eaten up with	PHRASE If someone is **eaten up with** jealousy, curiosity, or desire, they feel it very intensely.
kindle	VERB If something **kindles** a particular emotion in someone, it makes them start to feel it.
melting pot	NOUN A **melting pot** is a place or situation in which people or ideas of different kinds gradually get mixed together.
meteoric	ADJECTIVE If someone has a **meteoric** rise, they achieve success very quickly.
old flame	NOUN An **old flame** is someone with whom you had a romantic relationship in the past.
plough on	PHRASAL VERB If you **plough on**, you continue doing something although it is difficult.
plough through	PHRASAL VERB If you **plough through** something, you do it, deal with it, or move through it with difficulty.
sheepish	ADJECTIVE If you look **sheepish**, you look slightly embarrassed because you feel foolish or you have done something silly.
shovel	VERB If you **shovel** something somewhere, you push a lot of it quickly into that place.
slip by	PHRASAL VERB If time **slips by**, it passes without you noticing.
sour	VERB If something **sours** a relationship or situation, it makes it less friendly or enjoyable.
spill the beans	PHRASE If you **spill the beans**, you tell someone something that people have been trying to keep secret.
sponge off	PHRASAL VERB If you say that someone **sponges off** other people, you mean that they regularly get money from other people when they should be trying to support themselves.
swamped	ADJECTIVE If you are **swamped** with something, you have more of it than you can deal with.
be taken for a ride	PHRASE If you say that someone has been **taken for a ride**, you mean that they have been deceived or cheated.

Word Finder

Exercise 1

Complete the sentences by writing one word or phrase in each gap.

melting pot | swamped | meteoric rise | cloaked in mystery | downtrodden |
spill the beans | kindle an interest

1 My father was passionate about science and did his best to _____ in the
  subject in his children.

2 No one within the family talked about the circumstances of his death. The whole affair was
  _____.

3 His mother looked _____, old and tired. I got the feeling life was hard for her.

4 The whole city is a glorious _____, with people from every corner of the earth.

5 The late 1990s saw his _____ to super-stardom.

6 Essentially, I was doing two jobs at the same time and was completely _____
  with work.

Exercise 2

Match the words and phrases with their definition.

1 spill the beans

2 plough on

3 sponge off someone

4 draw a veil over something

5 be between a rock and a hard place

6 be taken for a ride

a to tell someone something that other people have
  been trying to keep secret

b to be deceived or cheated

c to stop talking about a subject because it is
  too unpleasant

d to continue moving or trying to complete
  something, even though it takes a lot of effort

e to be in a difficult situation where you have to
  choose between two equally unpleasant courses
  of action

f to regularly get money from someone else when
  you should be earning it for yourself

Exercise 3

Put the correct word or phrase in each gap.

eaten up | melting pot | an old flame | drawn a veil over | sheepish |
spilled the beans | sour

Apparently, Al was chatting with [1]_____ at Pete's party last Saturday. I had no
idea about this but a friend of mine who likes making trouble [2]_____ to me the
next day (she'd recognized the woman as Al's ex). I asked Al about the woman and he said they'd
just chatted briefly, but he had a [3]_____ look on his face and I didn't quite trust
him. I now find myself [4]_____ with jealousy over this woman. I mean, I don't
know much about Al's romantic history – he's always [5]_____ it. I have no idea
how important this woman was to him. Things have been going so well with Al and I really don't
want this episode to [6]_____ relations between us.

Exercise 4

Match the sentence halves.

1 He went to a reunion at the weekend

2 For two years, he doggedly

3 When his ex-wife started seeing another man, he

4 Rob was an appalling man. At the age of 54, he still lived with his ageing parents and

5 He had about five minutes to eat breakfast so he

6 Unfortunately, Oliver had no idea that the proposal was confidential, and he

a pursued his goal, even in the face of opposition.

b just shovelled it down before rushing out of the house.

c where he was amazed to come face to face with an old flame.

d unintentionally spilled the beans.

e sponged off them shamelessly.

f was eaten up with jealousy and could think of little else.

Exercise 5

For each question, tick the correct answer.

1 An old flame is
   ❑ a person who used to be famous in the past.
   ❑ a person that you had a romantic relationship with in the past.

2 If you do something doggedly, you do it
   ❑ with great determination although it is difficult.
   ❑ happily and with great enthusiasm.

3 If you kindle a feeling in someone, you
   ❑ make them stop feeling it.
   ❑ make them start to feel it.

4 A melting pot is
   ❑ a place or situation in which people or ideas of different kinds are mixed together.
   ❑ a hot and airless place in which you find it hard to breathe.

5 If you are taken for a ride, you
   ❑ are cheated or deceived.
   ❑ experience something that is very exciting.

6 If you plough on, you
   ❑ continue to do something that needs great effort.
   ❑ continue eating your way through a large quantity of food.

Answer key

1 British and American English words and phrases

Exercise 1

1 b	3 f	5 c
2 d	4 e	6 a

Exercise 2

1 cutlery	4 insect
2 number plate	5 casualty department
3 wardrobe	6 primary school

Exercise 3

1 cutlery	4 lift
2 main road	5 mate
3 property	6 casualty department

Exercise 4

1 insects	4 primary school
2 number plate	5 Maths
3 angry	6 lift

2 Work and jobs

Exercise 1

1 workforce	3 tender	5 supervisor
2 taken on	4 recruit	6 workplace

Exercise 2

1 entrepreneur	3 trainee	5 supervisor
2 skeleton staff	4 takeover	6 tender

Exercise 3

1 vacancy	3 dismissal	5 maternity
2 adviser	4 merger	6 security

Exercise 4

1 a	3 e	5 c
2 f	4 b	6 d

Exercise 5

1 sick leave	3 takeover	5 workplace
2 rewarding	4 recruit	6 trainee

3 Travel and holidays

Exercise 1

1 bound	3 move	5 give
2 drop	4 track	

Exercise 2

1 self-catering.	4 transportation.
2 vacancies?	5 track.
3 aboard.	

Exercise 3

1 eco-tourism	3 carriage	5 diesel
2 tank	4 launch	6 itinerary

Exercise 4

1 bound	3 trek	5 tank
2 commute	4 shuttle	6 diesel

4 Success and failure

Exercise 1

1 b	3 d	5 c
2 a	4 e	6 f

Exercise 2

1 an assumption	4 change
2 advance	5 feat
3 letdown	6 go pear-shaped

Exercise 3

1 expertise	3 letdown	5 potential
2 comes	4 loser	6 flop

Exercise 4

1 abortive	4 crash	7 fiasco
2 nothing	5 expertise	
3 thriving	6 prosper	

Exercise 5

1 feat ✓	5 get-down ✗
2 thrives ✓	6 comedown ✓
3 drop ✗	7 banana-shaped ✗
4 headlight ✗	

Exercise 6

1 fulfil	3 anti-climax	5 feat
2 climbed	4 ahead	6 headway

5 Services

Exercise 1

1 amenities	4 traffic management
2 multiplex cinema	5 courtesy
3 local authority	6 encapsulates

Exercise 2

1 is free.

2 the useful features that people can use there.

3 a formal word for a drink.

4 are polite to you.

5 it is a perfect example of it.

6 that allows you to spend more money than you have in your account.

Exercise 3

1 waste management	4 consumption
2 beverages	5 amenities
3 drop-in centre	6 extreme sports centre

Exercise 4

1 charges	4 fuel consumption
2 centre	5 watch
3 limit	6 withdraw

Exercise 5

1 hidden ✓	3 actual ✗	5 account ✗
2 enter ✗	4 facility ✓	6 provides ✓

Exercise 6

1 All our new customers receive a complimentary consultation with a personal trainer.

2 Upgrading to a more efficient boiler can help to reduce your energy consumption.

3 We want to design a new logo that embodies our company's innovative approach.

4 We try always to operate in an honest and professional manner that epitomizes the service we offer.

5 I was treated with unfailing courtesy by every member of staff I came into contact with.

6 Amenities such as good food, attentive staff and pleasant surroundings are all part of the package.

6 Register – formal vs. informal

Exercise 1

1 gutted	3 go ballistic
2 guts	4 repast

Exercise 2

1 e	3 d	5 c
2 f	4 a	6 b

Exercise 3

1 Yes	3 Yes	5 Yes
2 No	4 No	

Exercise 4

1 repast	4 negate
2 notwithstanding	5 denote
3 whereby	6 thereby

Exercise 5

1 gutted	3 grub	5 dosh
2 ballistic	4 scrounging	6 guts

Exercise 6

1 No	3 No	5 Yes
2 Yes	4 Yes	6 No

7 Feelings

Exercise 1

1 mischievous	4 threatened
2 grief-stricken	5 lovesick
3 sheepish	6 self-assured

Exercise 2

1 trapped	4 lovesick
2 indifferent	5 grief-stricken
3 hysterical	

Exercise 3

1 disbelieving	4 meditative
2 sheepish	5 bitter
3 indifferent	6 revengeful

Exercise 4

1 blissful ✓	4 self-assured ✗
2 mischievous! ✗	5 sheepish ✓
3 smug ✓	6 nasty ✗

Exercise 5

1 Yes	3 No	5 No
2 No	4 Yes	6 Yes

8 Education

Exercise 1

1 master's	3 nursery	5 feedback
2 grant	4 intellectual	6 journal

Exercise 2

1 faculty	3 kindergarten	5 crèche
2 journal	4 portfolio	6 feedback

Exercise 3

1 No	3 No	5 No
2 Yes	4 Yes	6 Yes

Exercise 4

1 statement	3 hall	5 maps
2 skipping	4 draft	6 submit

Exercise 5

1 c	3 d	5 a
2 b	4 e	6 f

9 Communication

Exercise 1

1	f	3	d	5	e
2	a	4	c	6	b

Exercise 2

1	demonstrated	3	jargon	5	record
2	making	4	getting	6	word

Exercise 3

1	No	3	No
2	No	4	Yes

Exercise 4

1 When we asked what he was doing, he asserted that he was carrying out a survey of shoppers' preferences.

2 The guide spoke only broken Spanish, which made it difficult for the South Americans to understand what was going on.

3 I don't speak very good Farsi, but I can generally make myself understood.

4 Can you put the record straight about what really occurred on the night of the 25th?

5 I have to take issue with you over your remarks concerning the directors' remuneration package.

6 You can take my word for it, no one by the name of Fitzwarren has ever worked for us.

10 Words that are used together (collocations)

Exercise 1

1	walk	3	detail	5	record
2	article	4	staff	6	attempt

Exercise 2

1 Unless the government gets to grips with inflation in the very near future, they'll soon be completely out of favour with the electorate.

2 The true causes of the resignation of the entire committee became clear when certain irregularities in the accounts came to light.

3 Joseph really relished the idea of going to the fancy dress party disguised as an extra-terrestrial.

4 A large number of well-wishers waited patiently to pay their respects at the memorial to those killed in the two world wars.

5 It can be very hard to come to terms with being made redundant with little or no notice.

6 The sinking of the fishing vessel claimed the lives of two members of the crew.

Exercise 3

1	genuine article ✓	4	skeleton employees ✗
2	pay his respect ✗	5	went under attack ✗
3	revelled the idea ✗	6	formidable opponent ✓

Exercise 4

1	vivid description	4	lengthy meeting
2	great detail	5	genuine article
3	personal effects	6	death toll

Exercise 5

1	greater	4	to terms
2	having paid her	5	staff
3	record	6	extinct

Exercise 6

1	Yes	3	No	5	No
2	No	4	Yes		

11 Phrases with do, get and make

Exercise 1

1	make	3	make	5	do
2	made	4	doing	6	make

Exercise 2

1	f	3	a	5	b
2	d	4	e	6	c

Exercise 3

1 have just enough money to pay for the necessities of life?

2 abolish or get rid of something?

3 succeed in a particular activity or career in which most people fail, for example acting?

4 spend a period in prison?

5 try extremely hard to do something?

Exercise 4

1	No	3	Yes	5	No
2	Yes	4	No	6	Yes

Exercise 5

1	do ✓	3	making ✓	5	done ✗
2	do ✗	4	did ✗	6	do ✓

12 Health, medicine and exercise

Exercise 1

1	blisters	3	syringes	5	blood samples
2	cramps	4	dosages	6	epidemics

Exercise 2

1	allergic	4	sprained
2	prognosis	5	blood sample
3	dosage	6	twisted

Exercise 3

1 vaccinations   4 operating theatre

2 syringe   5 prognosis

3 stethoscope   6 twisted

Exercise 4

1 nauseous   3 swelling   5 epidemic

2 immune   4 tranquillizer   6 cramp

Exercise 5

1 Yes   3 Yes   5 No

2 No   4 Yes   6 Yes

---

13 Entertainment and the media

Exercise 1

1 contestants   3 paparazzi   5 stalls

2 illustrations   4 sketches   6 gigs

Exercise 2

1 subtitles   3 journal   5 index

2 techno   4 playwright   6 cover

Exercise 3

1 transmitted   3 extras   5 dubbed

2 air   4 sketches

Exercise 4

1 d   3 a   5 f

2 b   4 e   6 c

Exercise 5

1 playwright   3 paparazzi   5 extras

2 shoot   4 telly   6 stalls

---

14 People – character and behaviour

Exercise 1

1 b   3 d   5 c

2 a   4 e   6 f

Exercise 2

1 courageous   4 conscientious

2 modest   5 talkative

3 extrovert   6 rational

Exercise 3

1 gifted   3 supportive   5 frustrating

2 stable   4 extrovert   6 anti-social

Exercise 4

1 distraught   4 informed   7 logical

2 genuine   5 talented   8 dependable

3 heroic   6 talkative

Exercise 5

1 introvert   4 modest

2 courageous   5 frustrating

3 narrow-minded   6 trustworthy

Exercise 6

1 No   3 No   5 No

2 Yes   4 No   6 Yes

---

15 Relationships

Exercise 1

1 f   3 a   5 c

2 e   4 b   6 d

Exercise 2

1 develop a close relationship with them.

2 understand how they feel.

3 They look after a child in place of its natural parents.

4 A legal union between a same-sex couple, granting rights similar to a marriage.

5 Someone who writes a magazine column, giving advice to people who write in with problems.

Exercise 3

1 strict   4 vow

2 extended family   5 nag

3 jealousy   6 hospitality

Exercise 4

1 no one will come between them.

2 for no particular reason.   5 we've formed a special bond.

3 a mere acquaintance.

4 you're driving me mad!   6 is called a single parent.

---

16 Computers, mobile phones and research

Exercise 1

1 device   3 an experiment / findings

2 come   4 installation

Exercise 2

1 b   3 e   5 d

2 c   4 a

Exercise 3

1 spam ✓

2 experiments ✓, answers ✗

3 clever ✗

4 unfounded ✗

5 compatible ✓

6 on ✗

Exercise 4

1 scan

2 device

3 installation

4 ªprogrammer, ᵇlanguage

5 up

6 case

Exercise 5

1 No **3** Yes **5** No

2 Yes **4** No **6** Yes

Exercise 6

1 it is not based on any facts.

2 Developing tiny devices at the level of atoms.

3 delete it immediately.

4 a particular person or situation is being researched and documented.

5 the development of organisms by the manipulation of their genetic make-up.

17 Talking about experiences

Exercise 1

1 in ✓ **3** of ✗ **5** as ✓

2 for ✗ **4** for ✓ **6** to ✗

Exercise 2

1 specialization **3** self-made **5** nurture

2 redundant **4** lifestyle **6** ambitious

Exercise 3

1 myself **3** redundant **5** highly

2 on **4** feel **6** showed

Exercise 4

1 raised **3** eligible **5** excelled

2 aptitude **4** outsider **6** distinction

Exercise 5

1 Carpenters who are self-taught may not necessarily use the best techniques.

2 Michael decided to retrain as a plumber after he was made redundant.

3 These specialist camps help to nurture the talent of young sportspeople.

4 Her specialization as a lawyer is in the area of copyright.

5 After ten years' service, employees are eligible for an extra two days of holiday.

6 My boss is highly ambitious and will do anything to get promoted.

18 Seeing, hearing, touching, smelling and tasting

Exercise 1

1 These cleaning materials are effective and almost completely odourless.

2 The photos were taken from a moving train and are rather blurred.

3 The berries are protected from birds by the shrub's prickly leaves.

4 When we reached the quayside the stench of fish was overwhelming.

5 There was a light breeze and the tiny waves sparkled in the sunshine.

6 We waded through slimy mud to reach the opposite river bank.

Exercise 2

1 odourless **4** appetizing

2 near-sighted **5** slimy

3 prickly **6** shimmer

Exercise 3

1 blurred **3** odourless **5** appetizing

2 harmonious **4** velvety **6** seasoned

Exercise 4

1 d **3** f **5** e

2 b **4** a **6** c

Exercise 5

1 rotting meat **4** smoke

2 figures **5** eyes

3 mountain scenery **6** conversation

19 Natural phenomena

Exercise 1

1 rubble **4** tectonic plates

2 relief operation **5** death toll

3 seismic activity **6** Molten lava

Exercise 2

1 aftershocks **4** rubble

2 sleet **5** relief operation

3 stalactite

Exercise 3

1 desertification **5** stalagmite

2 lava flow **6** aftershock

3 petrified rock **7** mudslide

4 stalactite

Exercise 4

1 c	3 e	5 a
2 b	4 d	

20 The natural world

Exercise 1

1 naturalists	3 erosion	5 extinction
2 Geology	4 habitat	6 extinct

Exercise 2

1 d	3 f	5 a
2 c	4 e	6 b

Exercise 3

1 earthquake	3 icebergs	5 palms
2 ecosystem	4 ranges	6 vines

Exercise 4

1 a	3 d	5 c
2 b	4 e	

Exercise 5

1 bacteria	3 spring	5 geology
2 ecology	4 straw	6 ecosystem

Exercise 6

1 geology	3 range	5 a vine
2 erosion	4 active	

21 House and home

Exercise 1

1 reconstruction	4 staircase
2 lounge	5 built-in
3 semi-detached	6 period features

Exercise 2

1 d	3 a	5 c
2 b	4 f	6 e

Exercise 3

1 period features	4 appliances
2 open fireplace	5 fitted carpets
3 beams	6 prime location

Exercise 4

1 mansion	4 staircase
2 appliance	5 lounge
3 period features	6 fitted

22 Places and buildings

Exercise 1

1 double glazing	4 quay
2 atrium	5 depot
3 reservoir	6 brewery

Exercise 2

1 an orphanage	3 dairy	5 depot
2 eyesore	4 barracks	6 reservoir

Exercise 3

1 a building, often in a zoo, where fish and underwater animals are kept.

2 a short road which is closed off at one end.

3 a view in which you can see a long way over a wide area of land, usually from a high place.

4 a place where children with no parents live and are looked after.

5 a building or collection of buildings in which monks live.

6 a small hotel or pub, usually an old one.

Exercise 4

1 panorama	3 monastery	5 gastro-pubs
2 setting	4 brewery	6 quay

23 Prefixes and suffixes

Exercise 1

1 bilingual.	4 countless
2 hyperactive.	5 changeable
3 invaluable	

Exercise 2

1 infrastructure	3 bilingual	5 counteract
2 outnumber	4 interactive	6 changeable

Exercise 3

1 invaluable	3 exhaustive	5 deodorant
2 hyperactive	4 multilateral	6 overwhelming

Exercise 4

1 humorous ✗	4 non-existent ✗
2 monolingual ✓	5 infrastructure ✓
3 disadvantaged ✓	6 conscientious ✗

Exercise 5

1 Yes	3 Yes	5 No
2 No	4 Yes	

24 Social and political issues

Exercise 1

1 liberal	3 status symbol	5 in common
2 peer pressure	4 anti-social	6 defence

Exercise 2

1 constitution	4 elder statesman
2 declaration	5 liberal
3 diplomatic	6 socialist

Exercise 3

1 d	3 e	5 b
2 f	4 c	6 a

Exercise 4

1 homeless.

2 don't share the same opinions and interests.

3 a cause.	4 the vote.	5 a deputy.

25 Words and phrases for linking ideas

Exercise 1

1 Rather	3 Whereas	5 Nonetheless
2 namely	4 accordingly	6 In short

Exercise 2

1 nonetheless	4 namely
2 correspondingly	5 thus
3 likewise	6 otherwise

Exercise 3

1 Yes	3 No	5 No
2 Yes	4 Yes	6 No

Exercise 4

1 f	3 c	5 e
2 a	4 d	6 b

26 Crime and law

Exercise 1

1 d	3 e	5 b
2 a	4 c	6 f

Exercise 2

1 perjury	3 assault	5 smuggle
2 manslaughter	4 corruption	6 blackmail

Exercise 3

1 magistrate	4 principal	7 perjury
2 assign	5 on board	8 corruption
3 collaborating	6 red collar	

Exercise 4

1 charge	3 on probation	5 white
2 serial	4 pleaded	6 detector

Exercise 5

1 charged	3 pleads	5 serial
2 mugging	4 probation	6 sentence

27 Talking about beliefs and ideas

Exercise 1

1 c	3 b	5 f
2 e	4 d	6 a

Exercise 2

1 diversity	3 atheist	5 dogmatic
2 believer	4 accepting	6 belief

Exercise 3

1 premonition	3 obsessive	5 dogmatic
2 overbearing	4 agnostic	6 ideology

Exercise 4

1 Yes	3 No	5 Yes
2 No	4 Yes	

Exercise 5

1 popularist ✗	4 mind ✗
2 ethics ✓	5 incredulously ✓
3 distress ✗	6 premonition ✓

Exercise 6

1 pacifist	3 dogmatically	5 overbearing
2 obsessive	4 believers	6 diversity

28 News and current affairs

Exercise 1

1 column inches	3 rag	5 caption
2 silly season	4 paparazzi	6 broadsheets

Exercise 2

1 a line at the top of an article giving the author's name.

2 the part at the top of the front page of a newspaper where its name appears in big letters.

3 an account of someone's life and character which is printed in a newspaper soon after they die.

4 an exciting news story which is reported in one newspaper before it appears anywhere else.

5 a short sentence or phrase, usually from a politician's speech, which is widely reported in the media.

Exercise 3

1 b	**3** a	**5** d
2 f	**4** c	**6** e

Exercise 4

1 masthead	**3** byline	**5** silly season
2 tabloid	**4** scoop	**6** cutting

Exercise 5

1 caption	**3** scoop	**5** gutter press
2 banner	**4** kill	**6** tabloids

29 Music and the arts

Exercise 1

1 easel	**3** sketch	**5** orchestra pit
2 score	**4** chord	

Exercise 2

1 lead violinist	**5** harmony
2 recording artist	**6** chords
3 instrumental	**7** applaud
4 masterpiece	

Exercise 3

1 Yes	**3** Yes	**5** Yes
2 Yes	**4** Yes	**6** No

Exercise 4

1 easel	**3** canvas	**5** score
2 harmony	**4** masterpiece	**6** chord

Exercise 5

1 easel ✓	**4** watercolours ✓
2 masterpiece ✓	**5** scores ✗
3 chords ✗	**6** sitter ✓

30 Metaphorical language

Exercise 1

1 kindle an interest	**4** melting pot
2 cloaked in mystery	**5** meteoric rise
3 downtrodden	**6** swamped

Exercise 2

1 a	**3** f	**5** e
2 d	**4** c	**6** b

Exercise 3

1 an old flame	**4** eaten up
2 spilled the beans	**5** drawn a veil over
3 sheepish	**6** sour

Exercise 4

1 c	**3** f	**5** b
2 a	**4** e	**6** d

Exercise 5

1 a person that you had a romantic relationship with in the past.

2 with great determination although it is difficult.

3 make them start to feel it.

4 a place or situation in which people or ideas of different kinds are mixed together.

5 are cheated or deceived.

6 continue to do something that needs great effort.

Pronunciation guide

We have used the International Phonetic Alphabet (IPA) to show how the words are pronounced.

IPA symbols

Vowel sounds

aː	calm, ah
æ	act, mass
aɪ	dive, cry
aɪə	fire, tyre
aʊ	out, down
aʊə	flour, sour
e	met, lend, pen
eɪ	say, weight
eə	fair, care
ɪ	fit, win
iː	seem, me
ɪə	near, beard
ɒ	lot, spot
əʊ	note, coat
ɔː	claw, more
ɔɪ	boy, joint
ʊ	could, stood
uː	you, use
ʊə	sure, pure
ɜː	turn, third
ʌ	fund, must
ə	the first vowel in about

Consonant sounds

b	bed, rub
d	done, red
f	fit, if
g	good, dog
h	hat, horse
j	yellow, you
k	king, pick
l	lip, bill
m	mat, ram
n	not, tin
p	pay, lip
r	run, read
s	soon, bus
t	talk, bet
v	van, love
w	win, wool
x	loch
z	zoo, buzz
ʃ	ship, wish
ʒ	measure, leisure
ŋ	sing, working
tʃ	cheap, witch
θ	thin, myth
ð	then, bathe
dʒ	joy, bridge

Notes

Primary and secondary stress are shown by marks above and below the line, in front of the stressed syllable. For example, in the word abbreviation, /əˌbriːviˈeɪʃən/, the second syllable has secondary stress and the fourth syllable has primary stress.

Index

façade /fəˈsɑːd/ 22
feat /fiːt/ 4
feature /ˈfiːtʃə/ 21
feeble /ˈfiːbəl/ 10
feedback /ˈfiːdbæk/ 8
feel at home /ˌfiːl ət ˈhəum/ 17
fiasco /fiˈæskəu/ 4
findings /ˈfaɪndɪŋz/ 16
fire brigade /ˈfaɪə brɪˌɡeɪd/ 1
fire department /ˈfaɪə dɪˌpɑːtmənt/ 1
fireplace /ˈfaɪəpleɪs/ 21
fit in /ˌfɪtˈɪn/ 17
fitted carpet /ˌfɪtɪdˈkɑːpɪt/ 21
fitted kitchen /ˌfɪtɪdˈkɪtʃɪn/ 21
flame /fleɪm/ 30
flatware /ˈflætweə/ 1
flop /flɒp/ 4
flyover /ˈflaɪəuvə/ 1
food /fuːd/ 6
for all that /fɔːˈrɔːl ˌðæt, fər/ 25
formidable /ˈfɔːmɪdəbəl, AM fəˈmɪd-/ 10
foster parent /ˈfɒstə ˌpeərənt/ 15
fraud /frɔːd/ 26
free will /ˌfriːˈwɪl/ 27
frequent /ˈfriːkwənt/ 6
frustrating /frʌsˈtreɪtɪŋ/ 14
fulfil your full potential /fulˌfɪl jɔː ˌful pəˈtenʃəl, juə/ 4

G

gadget /ˈɡædʒɪt/ 16
gastro-pub /ˈɡæstrəuˌpʌb/ 22
genetic engineering /dʒɪˌnetɪk endʒɪˈnɪərɪŋ/ 16
genuine article /ˌdʒenjuɪn ˈɑːtɪkəl/ 10
geology /dʒiˈɒlədʒi/ 20
get ahead /ˌɡet əˈhed/ 4
get angry /ˌɡetˈæŋgri/ 6
get at /ˈɡet ˌæt/ 9
get to grips with /ˌɡet təˈɡrɪps wɪð/ 10
get worse /ˌɡetˈwɜːs/ 6
gifted /ˈɡɪftɪd/ 14
gig /ɡɪɡ/ 13
give someone a lift /ˌɡɪv sʌmwʌn əˈlɪft/ 1
give someone a ride /ˌɡɪv sʌmwʌn əˈraɪd/ 1
give someone the cold shoulder /ˌɡɪv sʌmwʌn ðə ˌkeuldˈʃəuldə/ 15

give way /ˌɡɪvˈweɪ/ 3
give your word /ˌɡɪv jɔːˈwɜːd, juə/ 9
glazing /ˈɡleɪzɪŋ/ 22
go amiss /ˌɡəu əˈmɪs/ 6
go ballistic /ˌɡəu bəˈlɪstɪk/ 6
go belly up /ɡəu ˌbeliˈʌp/ 4
go pear-shaped /ɡəu ˈpeəˌʃeɪpt/ 4, 6
go wrong /ˌɡəuˈrɒŋ/ 6
grade school /ˈɡreɪd ˌskuːl/ 1
grant /ɡrɑːnt, AM ɡrænt/ 8
graze /ɡreɪz/ 12
grief-stricken /ˈɡriːf ˌstrɪkən/ 7
grieve /ɡriːv/ 19
grips /ɡrɪps/ 10
gutted /ɡrʌb/ 6
gutter press /ˌɡʌtəˈpres/ 28
guts /ɡʌts/ 6
grub /ɡrʌb/ 6

H

habitat /ˈhæbɪtæt/ 20
half-sister /ˈhɑːf ˌsɪstə/ 15
hall of residence /ˌhɔːl əvˈrezɪdəns/ 8
handbag /ˈhændbæɡ/ 1
harmonious /hɑːˈməuniəs/ 18
harmony /ˈhɑːməni/ 29
have something in common /hæv ˌsʌmθɪŋ ɪnˈkɒmən/ 24
headway /ˈhedweɪ/ 4
heroic /hɪˈrəuɪk/ 14
highway /ˈhaɪweɪ/ 1
home /həum/ 11, 17
homeless /ˈhəumləs/ 24
homesick /ˈhəumsɪk/ 7
hospitality /ˌhɒspɪˈtælɪti/ 15
humorous /ˈhjuːmərəs/ 23
hyperactive /ˌhaɪpərˈæktɪv/ 23
hysterical /hɪˈsterɪkəl/ 7

I

iceberg /ˈaɪsbɜːɡ/ 20
ideology /ˌaɪdiˈɒlədʒi/ 27
idiotic /ˌɪdiˈɒtɪk/ 7
ill /ɪl/ 1
illustrate /ˈɪləstreɪt/ 9
illustration /ˌɪləˈstreɪʃən/ 13
immerse yourself /ɪˈmɜːs jɔːˌself/ 17
immune /ɪˈmjuːn/ 12
immune system /ɪˈmjuːn ˌsɪstəm/ 12

impact /ˈɪmpækt/ 17
improvement /ɪmˈpruːvmənt/ 6
in a word /ˌɪn əˈwɜːd/ 25
in short /ˌɪnˈʃɔːt/ 9
in the same way /ɪn ðə ˌseɪmˈweɪ/ 25
in this way /ɪn ˌðɪsˈweɪ/ 6
inches /ˈɪntʃɪz/ 28
index /ˈɪndeks/ 13
indifferent /ɪnˈdɪfərənt/ 7
inedible /ɪnˈedɪbəl/ 23
infrastructure /ˈɪnfrəstrʌktʃə/ 23
inn /ɪn/ 22
insect /ˈɪnsekt/ 1
installation /ˌɪnstəˈleɪʃən/ 16
instrumental /ˌɪnstrəˈmentəl/ 29
intellectual /ˌɪntɪˈlektʃuəl/ 8
interactive /ˌɪntəˈræktɪv/ 9, 23
interpret /ɪnˈtɜːprɪt/ 9
introvert /ˈɪntrəvɜːt/ 14
invaluable /ɪnˈvæljəbəl/ 23
issue /ˈɪsjuː, ˈɪʃuː/ 9
it won't do /ɪt ˌwəuntˈduː/ 11
item /ˈaɪtəm/ 15
itinerary /aɪˈtɪnərəri, AM -eri/ 3

J

jam /dʒæm/ 1
jargon /ˈdʒɑːɡən/ 9
jealousy /ˈdʒeləsi/ 15
jelly /ˈdʒeli/ 1
journal /ˈdʒɜːnəl/ 8, 13
journalism /ˈdʒɜːnəlɪzəm/ 28

K

keep someone in the picture /ˌkiːp sʌmwʌn ɪn ðə ˈpɪktʃə/ 9
kill a story /ˌkɪl əˈstɔːri/ 28
kindergarten /ˈkɪndəɡɑːtən/ 8
kindle /ˈkɪndəl/ 30
kitchen /ˈkɪtʃɪn/ 21
knowledgeable /ˈnɒlɪdʒəbəl/ 14

L

ladder /ˈlædə/ 4
landing /ˈlændɪŋ/ 21
language /ˈlæŋgwɪdʒ/ 16
large /lɑːdʒ/ 25
launch /lɔːntʃ/ 3
lava flow /ˈlɑːvə ˌfləu/ 19
lead violinist /ˌliːd vaɪəˈlɪnɪst/ 29

panorama /ˌpænəˈrɑːmə, AM -ˈræmə/ 22

paparazzi /ˌpæpəˈrætsi/ 13, 28

parents /ˈpeərənts/ 15

partnership /ˈpɑːtnəʃɪp/ 15

pay your respects /ˌpeɪ jɔː rɪˈspekts/ 10

peace /piːs/ 11

pear-shaped /ˈpeəˌʃeɪpt/ 6

peep /piːp/ 18

peer pressure /ˈpɪːə ˌpreʃə/ 24

penthouse /ˈpenthaʊs/ 21

period feature /ˌpɪəriədˈfiːtʃə/ 21

perjury /ˈpɜːdʒəri/ 26

personal effects /ˌpɜːsənəl ɪˈfekts/ 10

personal statement /ˌpɜːsənəl ˈsteɪtmənt/ 8

petrified /ˈpetrɪfaɪd/ 19

pit /pɪt/ 29

place /pleɪs/ 30

plagiarism /ˈpleɪdʒərɪzəm/ 8

plate /pleɪt/ 19

playwright /ˈpleɪraɪt/ 13

plead /pliːd/ 26

pledge /pledʒ/ 19

plough on /ˌplaʊ ˈɒn/ 30

plough through /ˈplaʊ ˌθruː/ 30

point /pɔɪnt/ 11

popular /ˈpɒpjulə/ 27

porch /pɔːtʃ/ 21

portfolio /pɔːtˈfəʊliəʊ/ 8

pot /pɒt/ 30

potential /pəˈtenʃəl/ 4

power /ˈpaʊə/ 24

premonition /ˌpreməˈnɪʃən, AM ˌpriː-/ 27

press /pres/ 13, 28

pressure /ˈpreʃə/ 24

preventative medicine /prɪˌventətɪvˈmedsən, AM ˈmedɪsɪn/ 12

prickly /ˈprɪkəli/ 18

primary school /ˈpraɪməri ˌskuːl, AM -meri/ 1

prime location /ˌpraɪm ləʊˈkeɪʃən/ 21

prison sentence /ˈprɪzən ˌsentəns/ 26

probation /prəˈbeɪʃən, AM ˈprəʊ-/ 26

prognosis /prɒgˈnəʊsɪs/ 12

programmer /ˈprəʊgræmə/ 16

property /ˈprɒpəti/ 1

prosper /ˈprɒspə/ 4

punishment /ˈpʌnɪʃmənt/ 26

purse /pɜːs/ 1

put someone in the picture /ˌput sʌmwʌn ɪn ðəˈpɪktʃə/ 9

put the record straight /ˌput ðəˈrekɔːd ˌstreɪt/ 9

Q

quack /kwæk/ 6

quay /kiː/ 22

quote /kwəʊt/ 9

R

rag /ræg/ 28

raise the alarm /ˌreɪz ðə əˈlɑːm/ 19

raise your voice /ˌreɪz jɔːˈvɔɪs/ 9

range /reɪndʒ/ 20

rather /ˈrɑːðə,ˈræð-/ 25

rational /ˈræʃənəl/ 14

readies /ˈrediːz/ 6

real estate /ˈriːl ɪˌsteɪt/ 1

realization /ˌriːəlaɪˈzeɪʃən/ 4

reconstruction /ˌriːkənˈstrʌkʃən/ 21

record /ˈrekɔːd/ 9, 10

recording artist /riːˈkɔːdɪŋ ˌɑːtɪst/ 29

recording studio /riːˈkɔːdɪŋ ˌstjuːdiəʊ, AM ˈstuː-/ 29

recruit /rɪˈkruːt/ 2

redundant /rɪˈdʌndənt/ 17

relief operation /rɪˈliːf ɒpəˌreɪʃən/ 19

relish /ˈrelɪʃ/ 10

repast /rɪˈpɑːst, AM -ˈpæst/ 6

resemblance /rɪˈzembləns/ 29

reservoir /ˈrezəvwɑː/ 22

residence /ˈrezɪdəns/ 8

respects /rɪˈspekts/ 10

retrain /ˌriːˈtreɪn/ 17

revengeful /rɪˈvendʒfəl/ 7

rewarding /rɪˈwɔːdɪŋ/ 2

ride /raɪd/ 1, 30

right wing /ˌraɪtˈwɪŋ/ 24

road /rəʊd/ 3

rock /rɒk/ 30

rocky /ˈrɒki/ 20

rubble /ˈrʌbəl/ 19

run /rʌn/ 13

S

same /seɪm/ 25

savings account /ˈseɪvɪŋz əˌkaʊnt/ 5

scan /skæn/ 16

scholarship /ˈskɒləʃɪp/ 8

school /skuːl/ 1

scoop /skuːp/ 28

score /skɔː/ 29

scrounge /skraʊndʒ/ 6

season /ˈsiːzən/ 28

seasoned /ˈsiːzənd/ 18

seismic activity /ˌsaɪzmɪk ækˈtɪvɪti/ 19

self-assured /ˌselfəˈʃʊəd/ 7

self-catering /ˌselfˈkeɪtərɪŋ/ 3

self-made /ˌselfˈmeɪd/ 17

self-taught /ˌselfˈtɔːt/ 17

semi-detached /ˌsemidɪˈtætʃt/ 21

sentence /ˈsentəns/ 26

serial /ˈsɪəriəl/ 26

service /ˈsɜːvɪs/ 26

set the record straight /set ðə ˌrekɔːdˈstreɪt/ 9

setting /ˈsetɪŋ/ 22

settle /ˈsetəl/ 9, 20

settle down /ˌsetəlˈdaʊn/ 21

shadowy /ˈʃædəʊi/ 18

sheepish /ˈʃiːpɪʃ/ 7, 30

shimmer /ˈʃɪmə/ 18

shock /ʃɒk/ 27

shoot /ʃuːt/ 13

short-sighted /ˌʃɔːtˈsaɪtɪd/ 18

shoulder /ˈʃəʊldə/ 15

shovel /ˈʃʌvəl/ 30

shuttle /ˈʃʌtəl/ 3

sick /sɪk/ 1, 2

sick leave /ˈsɪk ˌliːv/ 2

silly season /ˈsɪli ˌsiːzən/ 28

silverware /ˈsɪlvəweə/ 1

sincere /sɪnˈsɪə/ 14

site /saɪt/ 15

sitter /ˈsɪtə/ 29

skeleton staff /ˈskelɪtən ˌstɑːf, AM stæf/ 2, 10

sketch /sketʃ/ 13, 29

skip classes /ˌskɪpˈklɑːsɪz, AMˈklæsɪz/ 8

sleet /sliːt/ 19

slimy /ˈslaɪmi/ 18

slip by /ˌslipˈbaɪ/ 30

smart /smɑːt/ 16